MANAGING UP

MANAGING UP

How to Forge an Effective
Relationship with Those Above You

ROSANNE BADOWSKI

with Roger Gittines

Foreword by
JACK WELCH
Former Chairman and CEO of General Electric

CURRENCY

New York   London   Toronto   Sydney   Auckland

A CURRENCY BOOK
PUBLISHED BY DOUBLEDAY
a division of Random House, Inc.

CURRENCY is a trademark of Random House, Inc., and DOUBLEDAY is
a registered trademark of Random House, Inc.

Managing Up was originally published in hardcover by Currency in
March 2003.

Book design by Erin L. Matherne and Tina Thompson

The Library of Congress has cataloged the hardcover edition of this book as
follows:
Badowski, Rosanne.
   Managing up : how to forge an effective relationship with those
above you / by Rosanne Badowski with Roger Gittines ; foreword by
Jack Welch.—1st ed.
      p. cm.
   Includes bibliographical references and index.
   1. Managing your boss. 2. Interpersonal relations. 3. Career
development. 4. Welch, Jack, 1935–   I. Gittines, Roger. II. Title.

HF5548.83 .B33 2003
650.1'3—dc21   2002035088

ISBN 0-385-50773-9

First Edition: March 2003
First Currency Paperback Edition: November 2004

All trademarks are the property of their respective companies.

SPECIAL SALES
Currency Books are available at special discounts for bulk purchases for
sales promotions or premiums. Special editions, including personalized
covers, excerpts of existing books, and corporate imprints, can be created in
large quantities for special needs. For more information, write to Special
Markets, Currency Books, 280 Park Avenue, 11th floor, New York, NY 10017,
or email specialmarkets@randomhouse.com

10   9   8   7   6   5   4   3

To Tekla and John, my parents in heaven

CONTENTS

A FEW MONTHS AGO, when Rosanne told me she was writing a book, I said great—as long as it wasn't about me, and as long as I didn't have to do anything for it. Now I've read the book, and it says plenty about me, and I am sitting here writing the foreword. So you can see who was actually the boss in our relationship.

Of course, Rosanne would never say that herself. The book you are about to read refers to me as the boss and gives all sorts of advice about how to manage up. Fine—I'm not going to argue with Rosanne in her own book. But the facts are, any successful collaboration between a boss and an assistant is a lot less hierarchical than it looks from the outside. For fourteen fantastic years, Rosanne and I were nothing less than partners. She may have been managing *me* up, and perhaps I managed *her* down, but most of the time we were both managing sideways, the way teammates do. We passed the ball back and forth, blocked for each other, shouted directives and encouragement (and occasional expletives), suffered together after losses, and, perhaps most of all, shared in the victories. I may have been her boss and she may have been my executive assistant, but it sure didn't feel that way. Maybe that's why our time together was so much fun. No question, that is why it worked.

Since my retirement from GE in September 2001, I've spent a lot of time traveling around the United States, Europe, and Latin America, to meet with managers and employees at all levels of an organization, in groups ranging in size from twelve to five thousand. I'm not a big fan of giving speeches—in fact, I haven't given one in years—so my main way of operating is to sit in front of an audience and take questions. Talk about energizing! It is thrilling to see how many people are passionate about improving their companies. In fact, despite the highly publicized cases of corruption that came to light in the wake of the stock market's decline, I am confident that most people in business are truly decent, honest, and hardworking. Any incidence of corporate malfeasance is despicable, but from all my experience, I am convinced that the vast majority of working people, from the mailroom to the boardroom, understand the value of integrity and apply that value as they help their companies grow and prosper.

During these Q&A sessions, I am, for obvious reasons, mainly asked about GE and its way of doing business. Rosanne talks a lot about GE in this book as well. But *Managing Up* is not just about GE. More than that, it's about being effective. I never had a boss who asked me to schedule ten meetings in one day, or get him from Pittsfield to Tokyo by the next morning, or juggle three ringing phones at once, thirty visitors a week, and five hundred e-mails a day. If one had, my foray into the business world probably would have lasted about ten minutes.

In this book, Rosanne covers every base. She describes exactly what she did to make our partnership work. Any assistant could heed her advice and make his or her boss burst from gratitude.

My only issue is that Rosanne leaves out three personal qualities that infused everything she did, qualities that made her even more effective—even more of a partner. (They're not mentioned, I would guess, because Rosanne is annoyingly modest.) Rosanne was—and any great assistant has to be—*loyal, discreet,* and *forgiving.* And not just a little of any of these, but a huge amount.

Loyalty is hard to interview for, and I'm not going to make the case here that I was even looking for it when I met Rosanne. I was trying to get a sense of her character, and I knew I wanted to work with someone who cared as passionately about GE and its mission and its results as I did. That's what I mean by loyalty—a kind of crazy, unrelenting zeal that makes you put the job first. The truth is, I did not want an assistant who thought of her job as nine-to-five, because I didn't. I wanted someone who lived and breathed work, because work was so exciting and important. I wanted a secretary so loyal to the GE way and GE people that she could read my mind, because she was that loyal.

You may be thinking that this kind of assistant is crazy. After all, what does she get for her loyalty? The boss gets money and prestige, not to mention all the credit. She gets long hours, short weekends, less pay, and little if any recognition. I would have to guess, however, that assistants who act with passion, zeal, and dedication consider their commitment—and its results—to be its own reward. When you care a lot, being at work becomes damn exciting. More than that, work becomes a calling, not a job. Now, that kind of loyalty may not be for you, but I've seen it in every great assistant I have ever known.

For an assistant, the quality of discretion is an absolute must, but I'm not saying that makes it easy. People in Rosanne's position usually know everything—from major strategic decisions to the most delicate personnel issues—and everything is what people often try to get out of them. You can't imagine the number of times I would walk by Rosanne's desk to hear her telling someone on the phone, "I have no idea," or "I really couldn't answer that." Her lock on information was airtight. She understood that even the smallest rumor emanating from her desk could and would travel fast through the organization, and in the process might even sink a deal or hurt a career. In thirteen years, I can honestly say that not a single word out of my mouth, not a single piece of paper or e-mail that passed my desk, was ever repeated by Rosanne—until this book, that is.

When I think about the importance of discretion, literally dozens of stories come to mind, but one really sticks out—the succession process for GE's CEO. For the last year of this race, as it was called in the papers, everyone knew that the candidates were three sensational GE executives, Bob Nardelli, Jim McNerney, and Jeff Immelt. The stakes were high, and not just for the three candidates. Many people in the organization knew the choice would drive GE's strategy for the next decade or two, and with it, many people's careers.

Needless to say, conversation about the succession process was thick and constant all over the organization. GE has an open, honest culture, but its employees are human. There was gossip about every possible "signal" from my office. This is not a criticism. I would have done the same thing. And many people pummeled Rosanne for clues; some people cajoled, others were pushy. They suspected she knew everything about what I was thinking, and they were right. But never once did Rosanne do so much as raise an eyebrow to indicate any leanings. With all the pressure on her, even pressure from friends and colleagues, this must have been incredibly hard. But the result was worth it. When the GE board selected Jeff Immelt, the process was as clean as you would ever want. There were no rumblings in the company beforehand, no leaks to the press. That allowed me to break the news to Bob Nardelli and Jim McNerney in the way they deserved to find out—privately and over a weekend. It also allowed me to tell Jeff the same way, with the added bonus of having his wife, Andy, and daughter, Sarah, there to share in the moment. And finally, the press was told in an orderly fashion, before the markets opened on Monday.

It occurs to me that I have actually never thanked Rosanne for this incredible, sustained discretion, so I'll do it here. Thanks, Ro. You are the nuts.

In the book you're about to read, Rosanne talks about resilience. She says it's important, especially when your boss is too busy to give you the time of day and you screw up on his dumb account. She's right, of course. Resilience has got to be one of the critical qualities for anyone in business—the ability to bounce back quickly, whether someone is being a jerk, the markets stink, or your biggest competitor steals your best customer. There is no point in crying. Get back on the horse, stick your chin out, and get on with the fight. Get on with winning. That's what business is all about.

I'm not talking about resilience, though, when I say that a great assistant is forgiving. Resilience comes from your head and your nerves and your gut. Forgiveness comes from your heart.

Overall, this book makes me out to be a pretty good guy. I hope I am, but there were plenty of times when I yelled at Ro for no good reason except that I was stressed out over a sensitive personnel decision or a tough deal going south. There were times when I blamed her for losing my keys (she never did; I always did) or for getting arrangements wrong (she never did this either). Basically, I am saying there were times I was a horse's ass. I hope they weren't too frequent, but I can't say they didn't happen.

It would be wrong to say Rosanne rolled over when I bulldozed through. She was firm with me—"Actually, you had the keys last"—

but never obnoxious. Then she would solve the problem—"Look in your left coat pocket"—which always put me in my place. A minute later, we would be back in business, none the worse for the wear. That's resilience, I suppose.

Forgiveness is that Rosanne never held my bearish moments against me. Somewhere in her heart she so deeply believed in GE and my devotion to it that she took my occasional bad behavior for what it was—simply being human. And then she let it go. Better than that, when I skulked forward with my apology, which I usually did within an hour or two, she accepted gracefully. And that was that—her wide-open heart never kept score.

Let me just say two more things. First, about modesty. Over the years, I have noticed that most great assistants, the ones who manage up the most effectively, are incredibly self-effacing. They never take credit for anything—from a well-run board meeting to a terrific judgment call on a potential employee—even when they should. Rosanne was like that. Of course, she doesn't mention that in her book, so I thought I would do it for her.

Finally, I want to tell everyone that, even though I am supposedly the boss, this is Rosanne's book. I read it before it went to the printer, but my only contribution was this foreword. Maybe that's hard to believe, given my reputation for digging into every project that crosses my desk. But after you read this book and discover just how well Rosanne managed up, you'll understand how her way of doing business made us truly teammates. This time, it's my turn to stand back and cheer.

JACK WELCH

FOR MORE THAN fourteen years, I've been a human answering machine, auto-dialer, word processor, filtering system, and fact-checker; been a sounding board, schlepper, buddy, and bearer of good and bad tidings; served as a scold, diplomat, repairperson, cheerleader, and naysayer; and performed dozens of other roles under the title of "assistant" for a man dubbed by *Fortune* in 1984 as one of the ten toughest bosses in America.

If I said that I loved every minute of it, you would be fully justified in questioning my sanity and/or my veracity. But have I loved my job? You bet I have!

In the pages ahead, I'm going to tell you what I've learned about surviving and thriving (while having an immense amount of fun) as an effective member of an extraordinary working partnership—and as a manager myself.

Hold on, that wasn't a typo. You read it right: manager. I believe that what I do for a living depends on the successful application of the art and science of managing up, down, *and* sideways. Managing and management are not dirty words, nor are they the exclusive property of those with MBA degrees.

We are all managers. Like it or not, each of us is plunked down in the middle of an organizational context—family, friends, neighborhood, school, job, whatever—that requires management skill to achieve a result. The flow of responsibility goes in every direction and uses different sets of tools to match the circumstances. But just as we are all managers, we are all support staff as well. No matter how exalted the manager, he or she plays a supporting role, whether it's serving internal or external customers, stockholders, or, in the case of the president of the United States, the American public and the Constitution. This duality has important implications. Managers and support staff are all in the same boat. The executive assistant is as dependent as the CEO on basic business skills, and the CEO rises or falls on the ability to do what it takes to accomplish nitty-gritty tasks. Both of them derive strength and success from managing this spectrum of roles, and from how well they support and manage each other (and the up, down, and sideways others). This collaboration occurs at all levels of every organization.

This book you're reading is a window on just such a collaborative process. What I'll be offering are slices of real-life experience on things that worked and things that didn't work. I'll take you behind the scenes at GE for a nuts-and-bolts perspective on one of the world's largest companies. In effect, I'll give you a visitor's pass and sign you in for a tour of areas that most people never saw when they came to GE's Fairfield, Connecticut, headquarters.

And I'll tell the truth about John F. Welch, Jr. I'm not going to give anything away in my introduction, because I want at least one person—his initials are JFW—to read the book, word by word, from cover to cover. But I do want to have a go here at the "tough boss" label. The fact is, we should all be so lucky to have a boss as tough as Jack Welch. Yes, he's tough. He's tough on mediocrity, tough on bureaucracy, and tough on dishonesty in all of its forms. Jack is *extra* tough, and the extra rubs off on others. There's a whole generation of business leaders who are a lot tougher and smarter thanks to being exposed to Jack Welch, and the companies they run are toughened up enough to stay afloat when the economy turns ugly or the market shifts.

In his early days as CEO, *Fortune* declared him one of the ten toughest bosses in America, not because he cracked a whip when he walked into the office every morning, but because he successfully transformed the culture and mind-set of a company the size of some small countries. History proved *Fortune* correct—he's tough, all right.

Does that mean Jack Welch is perfect? Infallible? Unassailable?

Read the book, then you tell me.

———

As an author, my goal is to give you, the reader, something you can use to build effective working partnerships without having to deal with theoretical bells and whistles or a litany of how-tos (which is just not my thing). Think of each chapter as a specific tool. I'll show how my colleagues at GE and I used these techniques to solve problems, develop opportunities, and, in general, navigate from Monday to Friday. Feel free to skip around. When you find a theme or an idea that interests you, plunge in. Seek out the material that relates to what's going on in your life, and perhaps set the other stuff aside. That's an example of prioritizing, and good managers do it every day.

In other words, as you read, let your instincts come into play. Suppose, for example, that you have a problem with low energy. Take a look at Chapter 5, which deals with energy. Or if there's a fairness issue affecting you or your staff, Chapter 12 may be useful. I'd like to think of this book as the equivalent of a can of Drano. Sink clogged? Dump it in, stand back, and see if the product works. It may or may not address your specific problem, but I'm confident that over the course of the book, you'll find plenty of tips, techniques, or examples to make you more effective in working with your boss (or working with your support staff). And if not, you may find that my fourteen years with Jack Welch have yielded plenty of entertainment value, at least.

Just a note as I go forward in this book: I've elected to refer to Jack Welch in many cases simply as "Jack." Personally, I'm a little uneasy with it because during my entire career working for him when he was CEO of GE, I, and most of the company's administrative staff, respectfully, professionally, and fondly referred to him only as "Mr. Welch." But as long as I've gone so far as to share with the readers the personal side of the man who captained our team, I don't think he'll mind if I simplify matters a bit by using just his first name. I never called him "boss" and never thought of him that way. For some reason it just never described who he was. And "coach" doesn't do the trick either, since I never saw him walk around with a whistle around his neck. So let's just go with "Jack" and leave it at that.

GUN AND GO

In May 2000, *Newsweek* dubbed me Jack Welch's "secret weapon" in a story about my years "alongside America's uber-boss." A nice compliment, but way off the mark. Secret weapons don't win business victories, foot soldiers do. Businesses and armies triumph when their troops show up every day ready to fight. That's what I did, and still do. In my case, one of the few things that really are no big secret is that I know how to create time. That's one of the techniques I'll share in this book. There's no precise and scientific way to estimate it, but I'd guess that I've provided Jack Welch with an extra twenty thousand hours over the course of close to fifteen years. That's the equivalent of adding about a twenty-four-hour day each week. In the search for competitive advantage, what could you do with twenty-four additional hours a week? Plan? Motivate? Train? Perfect the process? Implement change? Deal with customers? Read e-mail? Whatever the answer, I know that more time is needed—desperately needed—by every busy man and woman, whether at work or home.

When I'm cranked up, two hours of phone work, slogging through files, and reviewing briefing material will come down to a thirty-second "gun and go" item that hits Jack's desk. I deliver the essential elements of what he needs to make a decision so that he can make it and move on. I'm not doing my job well enough when I get a note back from him with a question that I haven't already anticipated and answered. Am I a mind reader? No. But I pay attention to what's happening around me, and I make sure I understand why it's happening. I suppose I'm a student of cause and effect, which allows me to make a reasonably accurate assessment of what sort of executive input will be required, so that I encapsulate it appropriately. The bulk of that preparation is information gathering, communication, and coordination—and it is the same for anyone attempting to be a briefing-material expert, no matter what their job description.

Simply passing along a customer complaint or issue, for example, doesn't create time. It is, in fact, a time sponge. Quickly, the inbox runneth over. Without support, the executive must stop what he or she is doing to find out what's going on, who is handling the project, and what's being done about it. Often, it means juggling priorities and diverting attention from more urgent matters. With proper support, the complaint hits the desk with notes or a memo covering those points so that the boss can be assured that the customer is satisfied, and can do what it takes to make sure the situation doesn't happen again. What might have gobbled up hours can be taken care of in minutes.

By functioning in this way, you've allowed your manager to skip over time-consuming preliminaries to focus his or her resources on the final outcome. I scrub every item Jack Welch gets to make sure it's free of nonessentials or of aspects that can be handled at another level. If I'm asked, "What's Harry doing about this?" the next time I hand him a similar document about an issue, I'll have contacted Harry beforehand and asked a few basic questions. Time is too precious to waste by touching a piece of paper, a project, or a problem more than is absolutely necessary. Sometimes high-touch is unavoidable and essential. But disciplined one-touch or low-touch provides an extra cushion that can be used to grow a business, or to fight fires that threaten to burn the operation to the ground.

TERMS OF ESTRANGEMENT

Since I can occasionally be a troublemaker, I will deliberately and somewhat provocatively use the S-word in this introduction. I started my career as a secretary, and I'm still at it. I answer the phone, place calls, take shorthand, type, and perform many of the other traditional secretarial assignments. But as an executive assistant, a far more accurate and palatable term, I perform countless traditional management roles—project manager, coordinator, communicator, troubleshooter, and the like. In effect, I am a hybrid of these functions.

A few pages ago, I said that we are all managers. We are also all secretaries. I don't care if you come to work in a chauffeured limo or ride the bus. We all act—or should act—in a secretarial fashion at times, rolling up our sleeves and doing the mundane tasks that make grand business strategies work.

And I can acknowledge, without blushing or fidgeting, that I've spent my career as a secretary. It runs in my genes. My mother spent all of her career as a secretary, much of it for a Bridgeport, Connecticut, lumber company. She was proud of what she did and was very good at it. Part of doing business as usual at Burritt Lumber Company back in the 1940s was for the secretaries to spend every Saturday morning at the office, without pay, writing letters of encouragement to American soldiers, sailors, and airmen serving overseas in World War II. Beyond selling quality products, that company knew the importance of quality community service. No wonder she liked her job.

The term *secretary* has lost whatever cachet it might have had at one time. Nonetheless, companies can't survive without highly trained, motivated, and empowered administrative support staffs. Call them vice presidents for STSS (sweating the small stuff). Whatever the term, I would argue these are the people on the front lines, and often the cutting edge, of every organization's basic "keep the doors open and the lights on" functions.

Business enterprises, and nonbusiness organizations for that matter, are complex undertakings. To operate successfully, many component parts must be integrated, orchestrated, and coordinated against tight deadlines and across times zones and national boundaries. Without dedicated and determined help, all the strategic thinking, careful planning, command-and-control structures, innovation, and high technology will fall short. Someone has to be there to simply get the job done, whatever his or her title is.

For example, much has been said in business books and magazine articles about Jack Welch's habit of sending handwritten notes to his GE subordinates. One of his goals was to remain accessible to the rank and file and break down the barriers that tend to isolate most CEOs. But there was a more basic purpose. Many of those notes were simply intended to reach out and offer a little bit of help—an idea, a nudge, a pat on the back—to men and women who were working hard to close deals, satisfy customers, or manufacture high-quality products. Even the notes with a rougher content, the ones that started with "What the hell's this all about?," were designed to help break impasses and to bring a resolution. By the way, I never ghostwrote those notes or faked his signature on autograph requests—he was truly his own secretary when it came to those.

Businesspeople drive themselves crazy trying to assign value to the hundreds of actions they must take each day instead of first determining whether or not that action supports a long-term goal. The reason there is so much fuss about using the term *secretary* is that it is encrusted by the barnacles of so many value judgments about the purpose of being support staff. We need to get back to the reality of the workplace: No matter what your job, salary, or title, if you're not helping, you're hindering.

The essence of management—regardless of your title—is making things happen. Does that sound too minimalist? Insufficiently grandiose? Not for me. In more than twenty-five years in various administrative support positions, I've taken enormous satisfaction from asking myself this question: Did the work I performed today help to achieve a goal? And usually the answer was yes—even if all I did was set a new world record for the number of e-mails a human being can answer in one day. It helps that I'm an *investor*. I invest time and effort in the things that are happening around me. I don't hold back. And that's another of the secrets I'll talk more about.

It helps if your organization—and I'm speaking broadly when I use that term—has clearly identified goals worth investing in. If you ask yourself the question I asked above and don't get a satisfactory answer, it may mean that you're in the wrong organization. You can find a new organization—or you can help to transform yours by managing up, down, and sideways so that you can ask and always get the kind of answers that make being a secretary, a manager, or a CEO such a joy.

That's what *Managing Up* is all about.

Principles of Managing Up

- Managing is not the exclusive property of MBA grads.
- At times we are all managers, and we are all support staff; managers have to roll up their sleeves and get in the trenches.
- Those who manage up have to think—and act—like managers.
- A good manager is a student of cause and effect.
- It's not good enough to be aware of what's happening around you; you have to know *why* it's happening.
- If you're not helping, you're hindering.
- Ask yourself: Did the work I performed today help achieve a goal?

CHAPTER 1

Chemistry

"WHEN THE GODS . . . punish us, they answer our prayers," wrote Oscar Wilde. In other words, be careful what you wish for.

In the fall of 1988, I had no interest in becoming executive assistant to John F. Welch, the Chairman and CEO of GE. In fact, from my job as administrative assistant in GE's Corporate Human Resources department, I was praying to get a promotion to an entry-level management position that had just opened up in GE Supply. In retrospect, perhaps my prayers conveyed mixed messages. On one hand, I wanted to move up the ladder, but on the other, I liked my boss, my colleagues, and the work I was doing. The two wishes may have canceled each other out.

At the time, I had been at GE for more than twelve years in a variety of administrative assignments. Corporate Human Resources was one of the better gigs, with lots of responsibility and opportunities to deal with senior executives and some of the company's hottest businesses. One of the advantages of being in HR was that it let you get involved in many different areas instead of being stuck doing the same old thing. I know HR can be dumped on for being too "back-office" or "touchy-feely," but that's a bad rap. A good HR department goes beyond handing out benefit booklets and is the driver of successful employee development.

The broad experience I gained in HR is what gave me a shot at the posted open management position. That job entailed managing a group of regional sales facilities for products distributed by GE Supply. I actively campaigned for the job and overcame most of the personnel hurdles. Jack Peiffer (senior vice president of Corporate Human Resources and my manager at the time) agreed to the move. He was a wonderful boss with a down-to-earth demeanor, and his blessing on my candidacy was important not only politically but personally. Nonetheless, I was having trouble bringing the final offer to closure, so I went to him to ask what was going on. Instead of giving me a straight answer, his usual approach, he tap-danced around, finally saying that on further reflection he didn't think the position was right for me. I was shocked and angry, and left his office determined to get the promotion or quit. Being single and not having children, I had—and still have—the luxury of independence and a few rash acts. I was happy working at GE, but I was not going to be stifled and held back. I wanted out. A few days later, Mr. Peiffer took me aside and explained what was going on: Jack Welch's executive assistant, Helga Keller, was leaving to get married. My name had been tossed into the hat as a possible candidate, and I was on the short list.

I briefly considered taking my name off the list, but I didn't want to embarrass those who had obviously been singing my praises. I was also curious to see what the hiring process was like at the CEO-level of a company as enormous as GE. Maybe I'd learn something new. I agreed to be screened and, if I made it that far, interviewed by Jack Welch. It may seem like a pretty flimsy rationale for not pursuing the management slot, but at the time it made sense to me. But I've never kidded myself into thinking that Mr. Peiffer and the company got out the scales and carefully weighed the benefits of Rosanne the manager against Rosanne the executive assistant. HR had a paramount goal: fill the position in the CEO's office with someone who had a reasonable track record and was likely to stick it out for a while. Jack Peiffer was enough of an HR veteran to know how tricky it is to match a senior executive with an assistant and how costly a mistake can be in terms of wasted time, aggravation, and lost productivity. A successful match also comes from pure personal chemistry. Filling the position of the executive assistant to the CEO was a more crucial task for HR than filling an entry-level management position at GE Supply. It was easier for the HR team to disappoint me temporarily. Looking back, if I had been in Jack Peiffer's shoes, I would have made the same decision that he did. Besides, I wasn't disappointed for long.

MS. CURIOSITY AND MISCALCULATION

At the time, I didn't think there was a chance I would get the job.

Why?

Because I really didn't want it. But I realize in retrospect that my "not a chance" mind-set gave me a tremendous advantage over the other candidates. I wasn't afraid, and I didn't overprepare or oversell myself in my one-hour interview with Jack Welch at a subsequent lunch several days later.

Also, the Jack Welch "cult" was only in its infancy, or more accurately, adolescence. After seven years as CEO, he'd had his share of media attention, much of it critical, or at least tough and skeptical.

At the time, the Welch cost-cutting, downsizing, and deal-making style was fodder for columnists and commentators, but at GE headquarters he was simply the CEO rather than a legend or icon. Jack Peiffer and the other department heads, whom I dealt with day in and day out, were far more immediate and real to me. Jack Welch was a blip on someone else's radar screen.

I'm probably going to regret these comments. But please don't misread me. Jack Welch was definitely shaking up GE. Yet at the time he was not held in awe by most GE headquarters employees any more than Reg Jones, his predecessor, had been. The glory years of GE's being the largest and most valuable company in the world were still to come.

While I didn't do anything special to prepare for the interview, I wasn't as lackadaisical as I sound. At that level and with such a large company, there are literally thousands of issues and functions involved. I could have crammed for weeks without scratching the surface—and probably wouldn't have really lighted on anything even resembling a surface, for that matter. Putting aside my underlying belief that there was no way I would be offered the job, it would have been crazy to try to bluff my way into it.

CEOs may not always inspire awe, but they don't rise to the top without being able to spot phonies. I'm not saying that being prepared is the same thing as faking it. Not at all. But the most impressive preparation is the kind that comes from being fully effective in your present job. It doesn't come from drills, dry runs, or dress rehearsals prior to an interview. Being fully effective springs from building a reputation for being a team player, demonstrating a willingness to accept responsibility, bringing new ideas to the job, and being productive. Knowing today what was at stake and how much I would have missed out on if I hadn't gotten the job, I might have done a bit more homework if I were to do it all over again. But even today I'd have to say it's easy to overdo it. There were several times that I've kidded around, small-talked, and tried to calm the jitters in otherwise well-qualified men and women who came in to interview with Jack Welch. What I couldn't come out and say was, "This guy knows your record and résumé as well as you do. Now he wants to know who you are. Just go in there and be yourself."

I know—easier said than done. In my case, despite not wearing a lucky bracelet or pulling an all-nighter, I did have the jitters. Worrying that I didn't prepare enough would have made them worse. I didn't shake or stammer; I blushed. When I realized what I was doing, I blushed even more. The red cheeks made a nice contrast to the blue dress I was wearing.

The interview took less than an hour. Then and now, the substance of it is pretty much a blur. He was in the side chair in the sitting area of his office, and I was on the couch facing a floor-to-ceiling window that bathed the room in bright morning light. Half of my brain was thinking, *Wow, I can't believe I'm sitting in this lovely office being interviewed by The Man.* The other half was saying, *Settle down and pay attention to the questions so that you can at least come up with a few mildly intelligent answers.* What surprised me was that he didn't grill me in that machine-gun style that I had heard about, which was a good thing because rapid-fire interrogation is indeed one of his hallmarks. It takes years of getting used to. A Jack Welch business meeting or briefing is best measured not by elapsed time but by QPM—questions per minute.

I'm thankful we clocked up a low QPM rate that day. Most of what he asked was aimed at measuring what kind of commitment I was willing to make to the job. He was obviously trying to find someone who could match—or come reasonably close to—his own commitment, which is basically expressed in today's lingo by two numbers: 24 and 7. I'm a hard worker and believe in being totally involved in what I do, but I didn't really understand commitment à la Jack Welch.

I do now, though.

During the interview, I was more than a little confused as to what he was driving at, and I told him so. I asked if he was suggesting that we do a trial run to see if we were a good fit. He dismissed that out of hand. He was not interested in trials. I was in it from day one—and so was he—or we could go our separate ways.

Then he dropped on me what seemed like the ultimate interview-killer:

"You remind me of my ex-wife," he said.

I was stunned into silence.

The best response I could come back with was "Doesn't sound too good for my chances of getting this job."

We both laughed. Looking back, I think what he meant was that he perceived streaks of independence that were characteristic of Carolyn. They had divorced the year before after twenty-eight years of marriage.

The way we left it was that at his suggestion I would spend some time thinking about whether this would work and if I was willing to make the commitment.

I didn't need to do too much thinking. I was hooked. Totally. I had expected a gruff executive barking tough questions that I couldn't answer. Instead I had found myself in a friendly, informal, wide-ranging conversation with a guy who, while being all business, wasn't afraid to laugh and speak frankly. I liked him and his obvious sense of purpose. Rather than scaring me off by pressuring me for a commitment, he energized me and pulled me into his orbit.

A week or so later, on December 2, I was invited to lunch in his private dining room. When I arrived, Helga told me that the menu of the day was spareribs with barbecue sauce, and the kitchen had run out of napkins. And then she wished me bon appétit!

Very funny. I ordered a small plate of cut fruit and cottage cheese. My advice to any job seeker at an interview lunch is that if you have to wrestle with it, pick it up in your hands, or slurp it, at best it's a distraction and at worst a disaster waiting to happen.

Our lunch turned out to be just a get-acquainted session to gauge personal chemistry. Six days later, I was summoned back to his office. Helga and Sue Baye, who was Helga's backup and processed the CEO's mail, were all smiles.

"Just go in," Helga said.

Jack Welch was standing beside his desk. "I guess you know why you're here," he said.

At the time I thought I did, but I soon found out I didn't have a clue about what lay ahead.

"Can you start on Monday?" he asked.

There's not much more to relate. He said I'd get a hefty raise, and that he was thrilled to be working with me. That's about it.

Oddly, one of the hardest things for me was to tell Jack Peiffer that I was leaving his operation. I immediately went downstairs and broke the news. He congratulated me with genuine sincerity. But I think he was nervous that I didn't realize what I was getting myself into. I cut it short, ducked into an empty office next to his, shut the door, and broke into tears. A few days later, at the department Christmas party, my friends in HR gave me a nice farewell tribute and presented me with a lovely gift. I sat at the table and cried again.

FOR CRYING OUT LOUD

I promised to share my workplace survival skills with you, and what have I offered up so far?

- Go unprepared into a job interview that has the potential to radically alter your life.

- Don't wipe your greasy fingers on the tablecloth at lunch.
- Casually toss around terms like *cult* in connection with your boss.
- And when the going gets tough, have a good cry.

These are all great words of wisdom, but I probably need to expand on the crying thing, since the other pieces of advice are all perfectly sensible and stand on their own. Dealing with stress is a major challenge in any job that matters to you, and on that issue I'm not kidding. On occasion, a tearful moment was my way of handling circumstances that brought on an overwhelming level of stress. It didn't happen that often, but when it did, I've used it to get things out of my system.

I have read just enough about the way the brain is supposed to function to know that tears release neural chemicals that help to soothe raw emotions and restore balance. Well—it's a theory, anyway.

After all, what are the options? Anger and aggressiveness? Passivity and sullenness? Obstruction and revenge? No, thanks. Find what works best for you to provide that momentary respite that lets you gather strength to finish the job at hand.

My way tells me that I still care and that I haven't been totally numbed into emotional nothingness by aggravations and disappointments. The capacity to care is a valuable gift. Business as usual—what a dreadful term—is the enemy of caring. It doesn't take long for the wrong kind of corporate culture to shrink caring that's the size of a quilt into a handkerchief.

There are other effective measuring devices, however. Jack Welch's preferred means of checking out the length and breadth of his and others' capacity to care was done verbally. He vented, ranted, badgered, and cajoled. And all of it was a sign of how deeply and passionately he cared.

The Welch style was totally infectious. If nothing else, as GE chairman and CEO, Jack Welch was an open invitation to care big time. He cared about people, about the customer, about GE doing its best and being the best company it could possibly be. And he continues to care. The commitment he spoke about during our first interview in 1988 was in a large sense a commitment to caring. It meant being willing to show up at the office each day ready to do whatever it took to make a difference.

TOTAL IMMERSION

It took a full year to get totally comfortable and up to speed in my new position. Much of the schedule was taken up by recurring commitments such as the shareholders' meetings, budget reviews, board meetings, and the like. My first year was spent learning how to go about dealing with these routine events. But because there were so many unpredictable occurrences, I would say it was difficult to master the job.

To step back a moment, it's probably worth noting that I was working for the world's most impatient man, and yet he was willing to tolerate a full year of having an executive assistant who was operating at less than 100 percent. Why was that? Jack Welch may be impatient, but he is realistic. It took that long because it takes that long. Sure, some are born with innate talent and instinctive smarts. The rest of us, though, need time to accomplish things through experience.

I had to personally go through a full year's cycle so that when the events and responsibilities came around again, I had been there and done that—and could skillfully do it again and, I hoped, do it better. Both sides of an effective working partnership, whenever you are in a company—whether you're a manager or an assistant, executive VP or CEO—should expect a learning curve at the beginning of the relationship no matter how smart and seasoned each of you happens to be. There is so much to learn, and things are mastered on the run.

One of the requirements they forgot to list on the job description was the need to be bilingual. My first real day on the job, I had to deal with the need to translate a "foreign tongue" into English. Jack was out of the office for the holidays and off-site meetings when I started the job. When he finally appeared back at GE's corporate headquarters in Fairfield in early January 1989, it was like encountering a human tornado. He came through the door of the third-floor suite so engrossed with a deal he was trying to consummate that he totally forgot I had zero miles on the odometer.

When he called me in to take a letter, I discovered that I needed not only Gregg shorthand but an immersion class at Berlitz. I couldn't understand his thick Boston accent. I sat there with my pen flying and thought, *Oh, no! I'm in trouble. What's he saying? I'll never be able to transcribe this!*

Meanwhile, he was doing several things at once—dictating a letter, telephoning, issuing orders, reading his mail, and scribbling out handwritten notes. In all my years of working, I'd never encountered anyone who could do five or six things at once and not miss a beat on any of them—I was amazed. Within a day or two, I knew that operating at warp speed for me was merely cruising for Jack Welch. Fortunately, I am one of the almost-extinct dinosaurs who still take shorthand. I had been the shorthand champ when I was working on my degree in secretarial sciences at Sacred Heart University, and it helped save me on my first day on this job. I could just about keep up with his breakneck speed. And I found I had gotten close enough phonetically to the right words that I could go back and piece together an accurate rendering with Sue's help. She had been in Welch's office since 1981.

I am sure most people feel like that upon starting a new job—

excited and terrified. Questioning whether or not we can adequately do the job is a normal reaction. What it really reveals is how much we care about what we do. Nonetheless, I couldn't help wondering: *Maybe they'll give me my old job back.*

As I was swept away by the human tornado, I remember thinking, *"Toto, I've a feeling we're not in Kansas anymore."*[1]

Chemistry Takeaways

- Be bilingual—understand and be able to use the language of staff above and below you.
- Good managers can spot phonies a mile away. Being a phony is a sure path to failure.
- Start building your reputation from day one.
- There is a learning curve for every new job. Expect it of yourself, and those under and over you.
- Work hard at being extraordinarily good at what you do.

CHAPTER 2

Trust

ONE OF THE FIRST lessons I learned while working with Jack Welch is that there is nothing more crucial to an effective working relationship than trust.

Trust is so important, yet so elusive, it's worth venturing through terrain that's swampy with banalities and strewn with clichés. Here goes:

To gain trust, you have to give trust. As sappy as that sounds—and it sounds like a gurgling vat of maple syrup—it's the basis of all successful professional relationships.

To gain trust, you have to give trust.

As one-sided as this formula may seem at first, it does not rely on having a giver and a taker. Both sides must give, otherwise neither side gets. Trust that is dammed up and doesn't flow from the top down cripples the effectiveness of a working partnership.

My very first job at GE was a classic case of trust busting from the top down combined with bad personal chemistry and a job that was painfully routine. I worked for the head librarian of the legal department's law library, who was extremely well qualified but came up short in providing a work environment that I could find comfortable and fun. I'm sure she didn't intentionally set out to make my workday intolerable, but we were coming from two different worlds. I was twenty, fresh out of college, and full of dreams for an exciting career. But I never imagined my dream would find me in what I regarded as a virtual prison. I remember my first day on the job. I actually started a week before my graduation ceremony and didn't even take a few days off after school was over—that's how eager I was to get the ball rolling. I couldn't have been more excited. Right off, I got the lay of the land from the woman I was replacing, who was moving to another job in the legal department. She pulled me aside and whispered, "I guess you didn't get the message I was trying to send you when you showed up for your interview. I could see you were an innocent lamb going to the slaughter. I was trying to tell you to run while you can, but you didn't get it. Now all I can do is offer my sympathies." My reply showed my naïveté toward that working environment: "I thought you were acting funny," I said, "but I just figured you were strange and that's why the boss was getting rid of you!"

During my time on that job, I was kept on an extremely short leash, but I wasn't the only one. The assistant librarian, a calm, conscientious, and low-profile woman, suddenly quit, worked out her notice, and at the stroke of five o'clock on her last day left without saying good-bye to anyone. She apparently couldn't wait to get out of there.

Most of my workday was spent typing catalog cards and writing form letters to law journals about subscriptions. There were five cards per book, done individually, and they kept slipping out of the typewriter, so many of them had to be done over and over again. To say that it was boring would be like pointing out that Olympic curling isn't quite as action-packed as snowboarding or luge. *Boring* doesn't begin to do it justice. For eight months, my ritual every Friday afternoon was to wait until two o'clock, go down to the personnel department, and beg for another job. I made a total pest of myself until they finally relented and found me something else.

At that time there was a policy that your manager must sign off on job transfers within the company if you hadn't been on the job for twelve months. Mine refused. It was pure Catch-22: The rule said she had to approve the change because I was on her staff less than a year, and she vetoed the move on the grounds that I must first work for her one full year. It was so painfully frustrating.

Eventually, I went to the personnel office to announce that I was going to leave GE. At that time, the job market was such that they had difficulty finding promising secretarial talent and didn't want to see reasonably good skills walk out the door. They found me a position in International Human Resources and promised to work out the departure rules with my boss. The interview and job offer came when she was on her vacation, which meant that when she returned to work she got the news that I was out of there and she had to start the process of finding another assistant again. That afternoon she approached me and said, "I suppose this means I should congratulate you," and with that walked away.

In retrospect, I could have learned to live with some of the boring aspects of that job. What was intolerable, however, was that I wasn't being trusted with anything but the most mundane tasks. And things never would have changed. But trust is like oxygen—you can't thrive without it.

WORK IT OUT

I would like to think that a golden era of trust and good chemistry has since dawned at every one of GE's operations. But I'm a realist: Problems still happen. Yet they happen less frequently and with less disruption, thanks in large part to the Work-Out program instituted by Jack Welch in 1988. Work-Outs were a powerful antidote to trust busting because they established an effective way to address many of the bureaucratic processes that weaken and destroy trust.

A lot has been written about Work-Outs, but I'm going to spend a page or two on them anyway just in case you need a refresher—it would be a shame for any business or businessperson to miss out on this useful trust-building technique. Think of it as a New England town meeting (that's how it's quaintly described in GE's public relations handouts) crossed with the Salem witch trials. Only it's not witches that are being discussed, debated, and judged, but hitches and glitches that are bedeviling the organization, its processes, and its people.

Work-Outs were a success because they forced problems out of hiding and into the open, where they could be examined, understood, or eliminated. The original motivation was to root out bad habits, red tape, and outmoded methodology left over from the "old" GE, pre–Jack Welch, which was saddled with many more layers of bureaucracy, but the program quickly became a mechanism for promoting change, creating trust, and tapping into the expertise of the "new" GE workforce.

A Work-Out involves ten to a hundred people drawn from the same operation, their manager, and an outside facilitator or moderator who guides the discussion. Eventually, customers and suppliers were added to the mix as well. Often, the manager begins by setting goals or laying out an agenda. The object is not to generate a free-floating gripe session but to target a few procedures or policies that need the most improvement. But managers don't get to stack the deck or declare certain things off-limits, like a redundant reporting requirement that he or she put in place. Frankly, a manager who attempts to steer the group away from a problem they feel really strongly about is in for a big disappointment. The moment he or she leaves the room—and usually that's the drill (though a few bosses stay for the duration)—the session homes in on the topics everyone else wants to discuss.

Since the facilitators are independent of the group, they see to it that there is a full airing of opinions, and they also ensure that a proposed solution accompanies every problem. The problem/solution format is strictly observed. Bellyaching is a total waste of time unless somebody can supply some castor oil. The rule is that 75 percent of the ideas must be adopted or rejected on the spot by the manager when he or she rejoins the session as it concludes. There's no filibustering or stalling. To keep things moving, any decision that must be deferred is assigned a date that requires action within a specific time frame, usually one month. This requirement really puts the pressure on management and rules out the possibility that the sessions will become all talk and no action.

Over the years, there have been thousands of Work-Out sessions at GE involving hundreds of thousands of workers. It has yielded an almost continuous stream of procedural improvements and, more important, a culture that welcomes change because changes are coming from the bottom up, from where the people who best know the work dwell. It's hard to be disengaged and cynical when you can tell the boss that you know something that he or she doesn't—and the boss actually trusts you enough to listen to your ideas and act on them.

I think the god of unintended consequences took charge of Work-Outs and turned them into a far more revolutionary program than Jack Welch envisioned when he introduced them. *Work-Out* became an epithet. Instead of thinking, *that's bullshit!* or just rolling our eyes and going along when we encountered a stupid policy or decision, we would shout, "Work-Out!" It became a code for "This is a stupid procedure that has no value, and I'm not going to do it just for the sake of doing it or because someone asked for it." Work-Out gave everyone the right, the duty, and the confidence to challenge just about anything from anyone that appeared to be a waste of time or energy.

**Don't be afraid to disagree—but
be prepared to offer solutions.**

And I mean anyone. Work-Out was sold so hard as a philosophical principle that few people at any level were willing to seem like they were advocating useless procedures and not playing according to the Work-Out rule book.

I don't think a single piece of GE paperwork escaped Work-Out scrutiny. Teams would pore over forms line by line, question by question, to determine if the information called for was 100 percent necessary. Thanks to Work-Out, we eliminated duplicate copies, extra signatures, approval levels, and all the other extra steps that make paperwork such a horror. This streamlining cleared the way for the digital age, which was hot on the heels of the Work-Out era. The process of going digital was relatively painless because, one, a lot of the clutter had been cleared away, and two, the GE mind-set became change-oriented. Thanks to Work-Out there was no need to hype the benefits of change and progress to a skeptical, status-quo-loving workforce.

The heyday of Work-Out is largely over at GE. There are now other hot management and change concepts that have pushed Work-Out into the background. Work-Outs still occur, but not with the same pervasiveness and zeal. One reason is that there isn't that much obvious red tape left. The proverbial low-hanging fruit has been picked. Today, when useless ideas are spontaneously generated, the Work-Out mentality kicks in without a formal process and knocks them out (most of the time). I do miss the war cry "Work-Out!" and the glee I'd feel when tossing a useless form in the wastebasket, as well as the guilty pleasure of using the same excuse to dump paperwork or shortcut procedures that may still serve a purpose but are getting in my way when there is work to be done.

Work-Outs are a form of power sharing that implants a sense of trust in the corporate culture and keeps it growing. They are powerful trust boosters. I can't imagine why any company wouldn't profit in a major way from giving this program a try. Trust me.

EMBRACING TECHNOLOGY—SLOWLY

It's puzzling, but in the late seventies it appeared that GE was a little slow to embrace the technology revolution. Lack of trust and lack of feedback may have had something to do with it.

By slow, I'm not referring to products and services as much as the so-called back-office uses of new technology like desktop computers, the Internet, and e-mail. I don't mean to say that we were slow to jump on the bandwagon, but at the time we weren't the industry leader, as we so often were. Partly to blame was the incredible speed at which new technology blew into town and the amount of change that was being force-fed to the American business community, but partly, too, it might have been GE's initial failure to trust those who were the first to see what technology could and would do. Jack Welch recognized the need for and the advantage of a strategic plan for our advancement of information technology and brought in a series of corporate leaders from outside the company who had the expertise to implement changes in this area.

Remember, in the mid-1980s there had just been a stock market crash, a recession was tearing things up, and the Japanese were encroaching on many of our markets. There was panic and a siege mentality almost everywhere. In a more placid era, I suspect GE would have been a technology leader simply because the demand for it would have flowed from the bottom up. Most people could see the technology revolution coming, and we all sat around wondering why we were being so dumb about not requiring the entire company to purchase compatible hardware and software as a single organization. The decentralized system for purchasing made it difficult to put together a seamless national and international network. The excuse was that each department, business, or location was developing its own methods to satisfy its technological needs. It was just too complicated, the official line went, to address everyone's individual launch into the digital age and incorporate them all into a company-wide system. Looking back, it was such a waste. Time and money were burned up converting many of those clashing systems later on.

This was in the early eighties, before Work-Out sessions had started. If Work-Out had been in place earlier, there would have been a lot more shouting at those sessions from people who had to retype documents because the software being used in Cincinnati couldn't convert documents that were being compiled in Fairfield—a lot more shouting, and a lot more listening and trusting that some of us knew what we were talking about.

As for adapting to computer technology, I was an "early adapter" thanks to my brother, Raymond, one of the first high-school computer nerds. Ray would happily spend his entire cash reserves on Radio Shack gizmos. He had fantasized about owning an Apple computer long before anyone even knew what an Apple was. He heard that a woman had won an Apple computer through a local radio station. Knowing the odds were excellent that this person wouldn't have a clue what to do with her prize, he tracked her down in the phone book, called her up, and convinced her that she knew nothing about computers. As a "favor," he offered to buy it from her at a good price. She was happy with the cash, and he was in computer-geek heaven. Although the equipment was primitive by today's standards, with Ray's help I was able to see the potential for producing pie charts and bar graphs by machine rather than by hand. I was one of the first people to bring that technology to bear on some reports we presented to the board of directors back in the middle eighties.

At about the same time, I was invited to attend a Coffee with the Chairman session. These get-togethers were designed to give Jack Welch a chance to personally interact with a small cross-section of the GE headquarters staff. We were expected to ask questions. About halfway through the session, I asked, "Do you think the management here in Fairfield is doing enough to keep up with computer technology that's available?" It seemed that Jack Welch did not have much of a feel for the technology that was out there at the time. He heard me out and said something noncommittal, like "We will have to do better in the future." Soon after, however, he and the company were well on the road to recognizing the need for advances in technology.

What moved GE forward was the general, from-the-bottom-up interest in technology that was arising out of the company's workforce. Management may have been slow to recognize what was happening, but any shortsightedness was ultimately counterbalanced by a willingness to listen and to trust those who had different perspectives. It didn't happen right away, but it happened. Trust got us to where we needed to go.

WHOOPS!

Travel and transportation arrangements are one area where I'd like to imagine I'd played a part in contributing a modest technological innovation. As late as the early 1990s, GE was still booking cars, helicopters, and planes from its corporate fleet for executive use by placing orders and confirmations in writing, or worse yet, by phone.

It would have been workable for a business with a stay-at-home leadership team, but Jack Welch was the ultimate roadie. And he was not taking a Greyhound bus door-to-door, either. A typical travel day might involve two or three different planes, several cars, and a couple of helicopters. It seemed like for every mile Jack clocked, I had to fill out a piece of paper or make several calls. The burden was enormous. I put up with this disorganized, technologically low-tech system until I screwed up. And I, for one, would rather manage up.

On this particular trip, the two of us were flying to Washington National Airport (now Ronald Reagan National Airport) on a GE jet. As the plane landed and taxied to the terminal, we rolled past a GE helicopter.

"What's that doing here?" Jack asked, peering out the window.

"I have no idea," I said, wondering which one of his staff had flown down to Washington—and why the GE transportation dispatchers hadn't told me so that we could at least attempt to combine our trips. I called the dispatcher to satisfy my curiosity and soon found out precisely what had happened: Our helicopter had been flown empty all the way from Connecticut because I'd ordered it.

In an earlier phone conversation with one of the dispatchers, I had wondered out loud if we would need the chopper for another leg of the trip that was under consideration (but later dropped). I'd been running through options, that's all; it was more of a conversation with myself to focus on what needed to be done. Taking no chances, he read my idle comment as a hard-and-fast request from the CEO's office, booked it, and set in motion a chain of events that a few days later would send the empty chopper on its way to Washington. The existing booking system, aside from being inefficient, had more than a few holes in it.

When I found out what had happened, I immediately told Jack and took the blame for the foul-up. No matter what the circumstances, it was my fault. I was responsible for his transportation arrangements, and a mistake had been made in conveying the instructions. I knew it was a costly error, but it taught me an important lesson: I would no longer rely on telephone conversations to reserve aircraft. The consequences of an error like that were not only financially wasteful but probably took a few years off my life. I resolved to develop my own simplified form to request aircraft in writing. Eventually—several years later, that is—the air transport staff developed an on-line reservation system that was even better.

It was about the same time that I kept asking the ground transportation folks to devise a system to reserve cars on-line. "We put a man on the moon twenty-five years ago—why can't we come up with a computerized system to request a simple car ride?" I asked our manager of transportation. I think the poor guy finally got sick of hearing me whine. He and a software team pushed to get the on-line system that we use today.

For the record, I usually stopped short of saying, "Jack Welch wants a new system in place." Over the years I tried not to throw his name around to get things done. Of course, people knew where I worked, and I really didn't need to say that he wanted this or that. I might have pushed a little harder than usual in this case, but I was consoled by the vision of the staff in the transportation office who processed those old carbon-set forms giving each other high fives once the new system was up and running.

THE ART OF CONFESSION

Jack Welch rarely got riled up about mistakes, at least those that weren't repeated. Doing business is an extremely imperfect process. Jack knew that mistakes would be made and that it's a lot smarter to learn from them instead of penalizing people for owning up to their errors or for having the guts to take chances that backfire. He built trust by trusting his people.

As you probably surmised, I'm not very tolerant of mistakes—my own mistakes, that is. I'll second-guess myself for days on end. But what I won't do is hide a mistake. I believe in full disclosure, and that's one of my reciprocal trust-building techniques. Implicit with every acknowledgment that there's been an error is the willingness to try to get it right the next time.

Admit to your mistakes. But learn from them.

Hiding mistakes—"moving on," if you prefer—short-circuits the learning process that often turns a bad situation into one where some value can be salvaged. A manager needs to know both the strengths and the weaknesses of his or her people—not for the purpose of punishing them for shortcomings, but to train them. Operating on the assumption that everyone is taking care of business—when everyone isn't—is dangerous. Furthermore, the architecture of most direct reporting relationships (up, down, sideways) doesn't leave a lot of extra room for concealment. I think that anything but full disclosure, even though it may seem well disguised, subtly and silently erodes trust. Most people have pretty good antennas and can tell when members of the team are smiling too much or jumping whenever there's a loud noise. If I start to feel a bit jittery, I know it's time to clear the air.

I admit that candor sometimes isn't easy. Here are a few of my favorite, time-tested phrases for breaking bad news:

- Before you hear it from somebody else . . .
- You're going to want to kill me, but . . .
- Are you ready for this? . . .
- It could be worse. . . .
- This is not as bad as it sounds. . . .

You get the idea: Suck it up and get it over with. The only concession I make is timing. I might wait for the most opportune moment to break the news. A few years ago, I forgot to send a check to the IRS, a mistake that cost Jack Welch a few thousand dollars. I had followed his accountant's simple and straightforward instructions to mail the forms to the specified address. Off they went. However, there was a second paragraph that I didn't notice, which said to include the check with those forms. If I had immediately come clean, Jack would have heard about it right in the middle of an important and hectic trip to Japan. I opted to wait until he was on the plane flying back to the United States. Good plan, except a copy of the IRS notice was sent to his home, so he got the news a little earlier than I'd hoped.

"Why didn't you tell me about this?" was the inevitable question. All I could do was sheepishly explain that I was waiting until he had finished with more important matters. "At least it's not a *penalty*," I added. "Just taxes and interest."

Admittedly, I was pushing full disclosure by delaying the news by more than my usual margin. More than eight hours is a bit much. As a rule, I will wait to the end of the day if the issue isn't time-sensitive. It doesn't make sense to disrupt the flow of business unless he has to make a quick decision. I use the after-hours formula for owning up to my mistakes and for the general run of the "it could be worse" items that are better handled when a cold martini is only an hour or so away.

To gain trust you have to give trust. I end by repeating this because it's so important. Of all the business relationships that exist, the ones between employees and their bosses are the only ones that are so dependent on trust that the smallest flaw or deficiency can potentially be catastrophically disruptive.

This puts an enormous amount of pressure on both sides. Good managers must allow people to act on their behalf and live with the consequences. In return, employees must adopt the established agenda and make it of paramount personal and professional importance. If those two parts of the equation aren't present, the relationship may not explode outright, but it's not likely to be as strong, productive, and satisfying as it could be, should be, and—as far as I'm concerned—must be.

Trust Takeaways

- To gain trust, both sides must give trust. Work it out— don't be afraid to disagree, but be prepared to offer solutions.
- Good ideas can come from above, below, or sideways in the corporation.
- Admit to your mistakes—after all, you're human. But don't repeat them.
- Make the agenda of the person you work for your own.

CHAPTER 3

Confidence

I WAS TERRIFIED. There we were at twenty-five hundred feet looking down at the sun-scorched landscape that surrounds Phoenix, Arizona. From my viewpoint, the expanse of beige, brown, and bronze streaked with the vibrant green of golf courses, turquoise swimming pools, and grayish cacti extended as far as the eye could see. Blue sky, silver wings, and silence. Not a sputter, not a hum, not so much as a faint rumor of the roar that arrogantly announces man and machine would once again triumph over gravity. Just an unearthly quiet.

And supposedly just another corporate perk.

Perversely, GE, the leading manufacturer of commercial jet engines, was rewarding a few of its employees with an outing that featured a half-hour spin for each of us in a glider. This "treat" marked the end of an October corporate officers' meeting, which used to be held at the Arizona Biltmore every year. I was part of the cadre of staff who had come in for the meeting and now had time to kill—or be killed—prior to heading back home.

In a sane world, a world without peer pressure, I would have stayed back at the hotel pool. But team building must be honored, even though the excursion was more of a lark on the order of a beer-and-bowling soiree than one that imparted useful skills and strategies.

I managed to keep my composure until Saul Milles, GE's in-house medical doctor, asked Frank Terpening, who had driven one of the vans to the airfield, for the car keys. Frank was about to climb into the glider's cockpit. "Keys?" Frank asked.

"Yeah, the keys—so I won't have to paw through the wreckage and get them off your dead body," deadpanned Saul.

When it was my turn, I strapped myself in with more reluctance than enthusiasm. But my stomach unknotted a bit after the little single-engine tow plane yanked us off the ground and headed due west. Or was it east? I briefly considered bribing the instructor-pilot, who was sitting behind me in the tandem cockpit, to per-suade him not to release the cable attached to the tow plane. But just as I decided I had enough cash on me to make it worth his while, the cable dropped and we banked steeply to the right and began climbing higher.

I pretended to be engrossed in the scenery, which I have to admit was spectacular and almost enough to calm my nerves. Meanwhile, the Red Baron (I have no idea what his real name was) explained how the pedals worked, all about the rudder, and how the control stick moved the nose up, down, and sideways. He was wasting his breath. I could hardly absorb a word he uttered. Then the pilot stunned me by saying, "Okay, it's all yours."

All what? Somehow he had the idea that I wanted to fly the damned thing. For a couple of seconds I was speechless. Then I screamed, "No, no . . . they made me come. I don't want to *fly* it!"

I don't think the pilot understood. The plane seemed to be going down as fast as it had been going up a moment before. Maybe he was having a heart attack. Maybe *I* was having a heart attack.

"Try it," he said.

"No way. Just keep flying around while I enjoy the view."

"Come on. You saw how easy it is."

"Was I supposed to be paying attention to those instructions? I thought you were just trying to impress me!"

He gave up, made several more slow turns to let me enjoy the scenery, and brought us back to the airfield for a smooth landing.

"How was it?" my colleagues asked as the Plexiglas cockpit canopy swung open.

"Piece of cake," I lied with a straight, slightly green face.

Why am I telling this story? To burnish my credentials when it comes to writing about confidence. I can say with certainty that you either have it—I'm speaking of self-confidence—or you don't. Confidence, or lack of it, has nothing to do with a taste for various forms of recreational suicide. I agreed to go up in that glider because I lacked the character to refuse. But I knew myself well enough to be aware that taking the controls would mean I was deficient in both character and brains, as well as basic survival instinct.

And why am I writing about confidence? Business books often don't spend enough time on it. Sometimes it masquerades as inertia, hypercaution, aversion to change, negativity, or a taste for trivial pursuits that keep everybody distracted rearranging the deck chairs while the *Titanic* sinks. Few of us are willing to say, "No, no . . . they made me come. I don't want to fly it" when there's a business presentation to be made, a risk assessment to be issued, or a dicey deal that must be approved. Instead, we make excuses and evasions. Whatever form these qualms take, at the root it is still lack of confidence. But I think that once we know what to call it, fixing it is the easy part.

Confidence is one of the more poorly defined words in the dictionary. Mine calls it "a feeling or consciousness of reliance on one's self or one's circumstances."[1] By that standard I was fully confident of the outcome if I had succumbed to the cajoling of the pilot; indeed, I was relying on myself to save us from a horrible fate. Nose first into a clump of cacti is not a nice way to go.

Developing confidence in your skills is paramount in business and in life.

Frankly, I can't do much better than *Webster's* at offering a formal definition of confidence. But I suspect that I have been in the presence of more raw and refined business confidence over the course of the last twenty-five years than most people, especially because I've spent half that period sitting about twenty feet away from the largest mass of self-confidence on the planet. Based on my experience, I can say that confidence flourishes when it is accompanied by five all-important elements. And they are:

- Experience
- Discipline
- Realism
- Perfectionism
- Flexibility

These five elements amount to a checklist we can use to determine whether confidence is being created, killed, or reduced to a thin and brittle shell of bravado and self-delusion. Simply being on the alert for the five—or, conversely, on the lookout for their absence—can make a big difference in evaluating your own performance and that of your team.

Good managers help to develop self-confidence in others.

EXPERIENCE

A well-run human resources department—and GE's certainly is—functions as a corporate crossroads. Over time, most every person and most every important organizational issue comes through the intersection. It can be a place where valuable experience—confidence-building experience—is available by the carload. I didn't know that when I bailed out of my first GE job at the legal department's law library. But my HR assignment provided a depth and breadth of experience that were equivalent to a university-level course in what it takes to hire, fire, train, compensate, and generally nourish the talent it takes to run a successful business.

Shortly after I joined International HR in 1977, they moved part of our department to Westport, Connecticut. As a satellite operation, Westport did not have its own internal human resources infrastructure in place. I immediately stepped into the vacuum and assumed a good portion of the local HR support lead, like providing pension, medical, and other benefit information to new employees, and doing the preliminary screening of job applicants for administrative positions. I even wrote the help-wanted ads to place in the newspaper. This kind of "freelancing," for want of a better term, is an excellent way to pick up new skills, widen a network of relationships, and gain a reputation for being willing to take the initiative. Such opportunities vary from company to company, but, as with HR, there are functions that can tend to be stretched thin, including public relations, sales support, and customer service.

As the self-appointed de facto HR specialist in Westport, I quickly discovered that I didn't have a clue when it came to not-so-minor HR duties like conducting job interviews. As it turned out, the people I hired—screened is more like it—worked out just fine and a few of them are still with the company, which isn't bad for a novice job interviewer. At the time, like any aspiring HR executive, I was good at explaining the workings of the benefits package. Coming up with insightful questions that would reveal the applicant's strengths and weaknesses—that was hard. Yet I can see now that I was instinctively following a cardinal role of savvy job interviewers: Shut up and listen to the candidate.

I was also following another rule by doing the HR work in addition to my other responsibilities, and it was a managing-up rule: Make life easier for the person above you. Busy with many other issues, the man I reported to, Bob Haughton, didn't want any part of those chores. He was delighted to have me take over, simply because it freed him from having to do them.

Make life easier for the person above you.

I've always been surprised at how reluctant many people are to venture out of a familiar niche. There are few better ways of gaining experience than volunteering to help someone who's been swamped by extra work because of a sudden crisis or a tight deadline. For an hour or an afternoon, you're exposed to a new perspective, new issues, and new demands. If you're not permanently buried in your own duties, there are many opportunities to pitch in to help other team members. Occasionally, I'd come upon pockets of morguelike calm with people staring off into space or reading magazines, oblivious to those in zones pulsing with activity just a few feet to their left or right. I felt sorry for the magazine readers. My motto—then and now—is "Better buried than bored." I suspect that boredom ruins more otherwise productive and satisfying careers than does overwork. Aside from being stultifying, boredom is a sure sign that you've stopped learning and growing.

Think about the last time you were thoroughly bored. Now imagine spending a solid eight hours feeling that way. Imagine such boredom for forty hours a week. Imagine it for thirty years.

Now tell me you'd rather be bored than buried.

Having worked with Jack Welch for more than fourteen years, I'm hardly the right person to propose a two- or three-year cap on assignments. But if I were starting out in today's business environment, which features such rapid and thoroughgoing change, I think I would be inclined to move from job to job more frequently. I'm not necessarily advocating hopping from company to company as long as challenging opportunities are present. Even so, it's probably not going to hurt your prospects the way it once would have when cradle-to-grave longevity was more common.

Sometimes when I'd get frustrated with the routine aspects of my job, I'd tease Jack by saying, "I'm stuck in this dead-end job." Until teaming up with him, I'd never stayed in a position more than four or five years. So the standard rap went, "Here I am after ten years [eleven years, twelve years . . .] in the same dead-end job. Time to move on." And he always had a standard comeback, which I believe offers a valuable message. He'd say, "I've been in my job seventeen years [eighteen years, nineteen years . . .] and don't see it as a dead end. As long as the job you're in offers challenges and room to grow, the time-to-move-on argument doesn't hold water."

**The job you're in should offer room to grow—
or it's time to move on.**

And at the end of twenty years as GE's CEO, Jack Welch was still growing. The phenomenal talent and set of skills he brought to the job in 1981 deepened and became more sharply honed with each passing month. When you're dealing with someone who starts off the chart, it's hard to be precisely quantitative, yet in my years with him I can say Jack improved as a teacher, a communicator, a negotiator, and an innovator, to name just four areas—I could rattle off a list that would fill several pages. He loved his job on day one and loved it a thousand times more the day he stepped down.

My own growth fed off Jack Welch's boundless enthusiasm. I am faster, steadier, and a better problem solver and improviser than I was in 1989. Why? Jack Welch had enough confidence in me to step back and go with the solutions and improvisations that I came up with. I couldn't help but grow.

As far as I'm concerned, "Take care of it" are four magic words that build confidence, and Jack said them all the time. If they hear them often enough, soon everyone starts saying to themselves, "I'll take care of it." In that subtle shift, a mere ripple of syntax, there's a world of growth and confidence. To those who aspire to manage up, repeat after me: "I'll take care of it."

DISCIPLINE

When I'm asked about how to build self-confidence, I think of a variation on the old, old joke about Carnegie Hall: A couple of tourists are wandering around midtown Manhattan trying to find the legendary concert hall. They are hopelessly lost, but in the right neighborhood; they stop a famous German conductor of classical music to ask for directions. "How do we get to Carnegie Hall?" they inquire. The maestro, true to his prickly reputation and flamboyant style, gives them a withering glance and shouts, "Practice, practice, practice!"

How do you develop self-confidence? Discipline, discipline, discipline.

Without discipline, a busy employee, manager, or top executive is fated for disaster. By discipline, I mean a stubborn and dogged determination to close the loop no matter what happens to get in the way of that closure. You can't procrastinate or fail to follow through—it's the kiss of death.

I've never kept a to-do list, because list making quickly takes on a life of its own that eats into the time that should be spent disposing of the items that end up on the list. Prioritizing all work is important, but spending a lot of time on documenting it, to me, was a time waster. By utilizing an immediate follow-through policy, I've eliminated the need for a list to keep on top of things and I never have to spend time on this sort of time-consuming prioritizing. Ranking and stacking your work—greater importance takes precedence over lesser importance—is not always a smart idea. Inevitably, underrated and undervalued items sink toward the bottom of the pile where they're forgotten until their disappearance touches off a crisis. Besides, ranking what's important and what's not is entirely subjective. Your assessment could be dead wrong.

Ninety-eight percent of any job is follow-through.

Ninety-eight percent of any job is follow-through, and 98 percent of problems are related to lack of follow-through. By shortening the umbilical between the initiating request and the appropriate action, you can cut way down on the whoops factor that plagues many operations. A ten-minute rule is very helpful. Set a tight time limit on when to initiate action. Better yet, use a five- or three-minute rule. Challenge yourself to immediately pick up the phone or crank out an e-mail. Once you discover how much your effectiveness and productivity have increased compared to those who don't use the ten-minute rule, I guarantee your self-confidence will skyrocket.

Another rule I'm partial to is: Never touch a piece of paper twice. I don't recall who came up with it, but it works well. The idea is that no matter what level of importance the paper represents, the moment you pick it up it gets dealt with immediately. You never have to reread a paper or readdress the issue again. Of course, I have to admit that as hard as I've tried not to, I did touch paper more than once at times simply because more time-sensitive matters came up. But the general rule still applies.

In instances where follow-ups to the follow-up are necessary, I open a file—yes, an old-fashioned, labeled manila file folder—and keep it on my desk ready to receive the goods: data, confirmations, related documents, or whatever signifies that the task has been completed. An empty file folder is like a ticking time bomb as far as I'm concerned. I have no compunctions about calling again and saying, "Jim promised to get back to me on this and I haven't heard from him yet." Chances are Jim doesn't follow the ten-minute rule, but to keep me from calling him a third time, he might opt to respond in an hour or so.

As a matter of fact, my ten-minute rule was the mirror image of Jack Welch's ten-second rule. That's how fast he wanted action. In comparison, I was actually the slowpoke. Fortunately, I was able to bridge the difference between Jack time and Rosanne time by the simple expedient of explaining to him why another nine minutes and fifty seconds would be required before what he was seeking hit his desk. Usually he was satisfied knowing that the wheels were turning. Most of the time, however, I was zooming along to meet his ten-second rule whenever possible or, better yet, to one-up him and deliver in nine seconds.

But believe it or not, I've always had to fight a tendency to procrastinate. Like many people, I'd just as soon put off jobs that I don't enjoy or that may lead to conflict and turmoil. My solution is to be on the lookout for my telltale signs of stalling, such as an empty file folder that has been waiting too long for the second follow-up call or a piece of paper that keeps being moved around my desk for several hours or days. When I realize procrastination is becoming an issue, I act immediately. No more excuses. Get it over with and do it.

Procrastination can be an insidious drain on one's emotional resources. I've caught someone I know well—me—mentally rehearsing for a potentially sticky phone call, and of course when I actually made the call, what I'd imagined was not close to reality. The rehearsal was a total waste of time. Those few seconds are better spent in some other productive way. I've never let this get out of hand; if I had, managing up would have been impossible. I've never known Jack Welch to procrastinate, even when it comes to having a conversation with a subordinate about subpar performance, a chore that many managers dread and tend to delay as long as possible. It's never easy, but postponement only increases the potential damage to the organization and delays remedial action that could save an employee's job.

For me, the backbone of discipline—and therefore one of the mainstays of confidence—is establishing a routine and sticking to it. For fourteen years, my first business of the day was to download the overnight ratings for NBC from the Nielsen service. It's safe to say that of all of the businesses acquired by GE during his tenure as chairman, Jack Welch regarded NBC as his special pet. That doesn't mean that he let favoritism affect his business judgment. In some ways he was more vigilant and demanding of Bob Wright, the network's CEO, and the rest of the NBC executive team. One sign of this was Jack's habit of asking for the ratings the moment he walked in the door. It was a ritual he observed from my early days on the job till the day he retired. (After retirement he backed off somewhat, but he still kept an interest.)

"Good morning. . . . Where are the ratings?" was his standard daily greeting. More often than not it was just "Where are the ratings?" Only a company-wide computer crash would have stopped me from having the numbers ready to hand over to him. The funny thing is that the ratings could have been great or terrible and Jack might have just shrugged them off and turned immediately to other things. He didn't try to micromanage NBC, despite his genuine interest in the network. Yet some mornings he would get on the phone right away to Bob Wright to congratulate him and the organization for a particularly strong showing or to offer observations for improving the entertainment programming. *Observations* is the softest term I can come up with, since Federal Communications Commission rules prohibited GE from interfering with the network's programming.

Beyond a little stargazing, which many of us, Jack Welch included, indulge in from time to time, there was a good business reason for closely following the ratings. It was a means not only of keeping score against the competition but of assessing the network's revenue stream. The higher the ratings, the more NBC can charge for advertising time. A projection is made for each show that estimates the likely number of viewers, and the ad price is set accordingly. If the ratings fall short of the forecast, what NBC takes in per minute is curtailed. The daily ratings watch gave Jack an ongoing snapshot of the bottom line. Why the interest in NBC ratings and not a similar measurement of other GE businesses, like air miles flown by our jet engines or the power output of our gas turbines? A one-word answer: *Seinfeld*. *Seinfeld*'s ratings, and the rest of NBC's prime-time lineup, sparked more human interest than a megawatt-per-hour calculation. While those figures were available and closely monitored, gas turbines just weren't as exciting. It was just a fun way to start the day and had no reflection on the degree of interest he took in one business over another.

I usually had time before Jack arrived in the morning to take a quick general look at the overnight e-mail. I'd sort out and flag the most urgent, time-sensitive pieces, and dump the spam and other time-wasters, like internal announcements about the GE parking lot or housekeeping items that he certainly didn't need to see. E-mail that I knew would need a considered response (research into the background of a problem, a customer inquiry, a request for a meeting, or the like) would be shunted from his mailbox to mine, where I could work on it before routing it back to him along with the appropriate follow-up information to include in the reply. We got hundreds of pieces of e-mail each day. After quickly scanning the contents, most of it I forwarded elsewhere within GE, and Jack was never aware that these items had once been in his mailbox. But, of course, for those with the slightest degree of potential CEO-level importance or the faintest tinge of possible interest, I would either send him a quick one- or two-line note summarizing the content and how it had been handled, or I would leave the original in his in-box.

In this way, I could cull through a pile of fifty to a hundred e-mails and reduce it to a manageable fifteen or twenty items. The routine also gave me a bit of a clue as to how the day was going to shape up based on any bombshells that came in. If there was time, I'd start pulling together whatever data he would require or alerting the right people that we'd need their help pronto. Agendas at that level are never set in stone, and my morning e-mail routine amounted to a quick rewrite or update to account for developments that had been unforeseen as little as ten or twelve hours earlier.

How did I know what would be needed and whom to call after going through the mail and e-mail? Experience and knowing the players. It probably took me a year or more on the job paying close attention to the usual suspects, the people who were the day-to-day players, to figure out whom Jack tended to rely on. Also, GE's structure is such that with more than twenty different operating entities, each with strong and accountable management teams, a lot of guesswork and uncertainty were eliminated. Based on the content of the message, I could reasonably pick up the phone to call the president of GE Capital, GE Aircraft Engines, or someone else to alert them that they might want to get their ducks in a row—and in some cases round up their ducks in the first place. By doing so, I was in effect functioning in a premanagement role. Rather than having Jack Welch make a cold call to those executives, in the interest of time and efficiency, I did the cold call and handled the preliminaries to allow them to be more prepared and effective when it came time to discuss the situation with him.

Most businesses do the same things over and over again. It's particularly true of manufacturing enterprises. There may be moments of creativity and the unexpected may occur, but more often than not, most of what's happening involves pumping out another refrigerator or more lighting products. Even the service or information industries tend to be basically repetitious. Rather than treat this fact as dull and boring, I regard it as a great advantage to managers at all levels. Repetition and routine provide a framework, coherence, and predictability. The patterns that emerge allow you to learn, refine, and perfect the process.

Without my early morning routine—not to mention the midmorning, midday, midafternoon, late afternoon, early evening, and late evening routines—I would have gone bonkers. Manage *up*? I wouldn't have been able to manage *me*. The discipline to devise a routine and execute it is essential.

Develop a routine and execute it.

REALISM, PERFECTIONISM, AND FLEXIBILITY

A healthy dose of realism goes a long way toward building confidence. It's good for the ego to imagine that you're engaged in an extremely difficult, demanding, one-of-a-kind quest for truth, justice, and the American way. And some of us are. But most people have plain old jobs. They may be rewarding and fulfilling, they may be fun and challenging, but most of the work we do—to use the old cliché—isn't brain surgery. Recognizing this reality, however, shouldn't foster cynicism and poor morale; rather, it's liberating and confirms that whatever tasks come our way, we will be more than capable of rising to the occasion.

Sure, some people are involved in complex scientific and technical specialties that require years of training and experience, but I'm talking about the other stuff that's done to run any business, keep the customer happy, and make a profit. It doesn't take a genius to master those skills. Common sense, planning, and perseverance are called for. If you choose to define that as genius, go ahead. My message here is that an average person can do this work successfully.

It helps, however, to be a perfectionist. A disciplined, realistic, and flexible perfectionist. The way I do it is to set out with the goal of creating a zero-defect environment, knowing that I will fail because I'm juggling too many jobs and trying to keep too many different pieces in play. Nonetheless, the effort will get me closer to perfection than if I had set my sights lower. Later, a little flexibility comes into play to close the gap between imperfection and perfection. Mostly, you'll find that flexibility comes in the form of quickly fixing the problem or working around it. In the end, one of the best ways to build confidence is to know that when somebody or something breaks up a key play, you're fast enough and smart enough to improvise and score.

Confidence Takeaways

- Get experience any way you can.
- Take care of what needs to get done.
- Show initiative, even if it's not your job.
- Always, always, always follow through.
- Relax, it's not brain surgery (unless you're a brain surgeon).
- Prioritize—then do it all.
- Roll with the punches when the unexpected happens.
- Fix whatever problems crop up as they occur.

CHAPTER 4

Impatience

ONE OF THESE DAYS it's bound to happen. You may even read about it in the newspaper.

Police Apprehend Aide to Former GE Chairman
Fleeing Fairfield Fast-Food Outlet
"She Just Came at Me," Victim Reports

One minute I'll be standing at the counter of my local Boston Market waiting to pick up roast chicken, creamed spinach, and potatoes; the next, I will have vaulted to the other side of the counter, pushed the girl aside, grabbed a serving spoon, dished up the order myself, sealed the plastic containers, bagged them, rung up the sale on the cash register, paid, made change, and left. The cruiser will pull me over two miles down the road.

A plea of temporary insanity probably won't work. I wonder if I'll be able to get away with temporary impatience? Only I fear the condition is permanent as a result of prolonged exposure to Jack Welch.

Impatience is a virtue.

Although I've evolved from a relatively easygoing person to a potential Boston Market hijacker, I am a study in patience compared to Jack. He wanted what he wanted—instantly. The normal gap between a question and an answer, for example, was shaved down to nanoseconds, or so it seemed. A couple of times a day he would ask, "What's the stock doing?" Although he had a diverse personal portfolio, GE was *the* stock of interest. Before technology improved, I would have had to dial up a broker to get the latest statistics. Direct on-line access changed all that. Even so, nothing is instantaneous. One would think I was getting the answer rather quickly—it took three or four seconds to call up the program. But halfway through the process I'd hear, "Well, what is it?"

If I still didn't have the stock quotation on my screen, I learned not to ignore the question. Silence would only draw another comment: "What's taking so long?" Usually I'd say—actually, I was shouting from my desk into his office, because Jack never used an intercom—"Just a second, the computer is slow." Of course, that was a lie. The computer was blazingly fast.

And so it went. I had a state-of-the-art electronic Rolodex on my computer that gave me almost instant access to 3,040 names and addresses. But *almost* instant wasn't good enough.

"Ro, get me Steve Johnson."

If I happened to be in the middle of another call, there was a slight delay while I either hung up or put them on hold.

"Ro!"

"I'm getting it." My Rolodex had an impressive array of features, but it took three or four seconds to launch. Mostly, it was a matter of clicking on the icon and typing the first few letters of the last name into the box that appeared. Meanwhile, I dialed 9 for an outside line, 1 for long distance, and sometimes the area code to get a jump on things while the main number rolled up. I hit on this technique when I realized that sheer speed wasn't enough. I learned to look for the creases or pauses in the program where I could get a head start on the next step. If you work for an impatient person, it's worth trying.

"Got Johnson for me?"

"I'm dialing!" Being snippy usually had no effect. When I got really sarcastic, he'd throttle back a little, sensing that I was exasperated with him. But the throttling back was infinitesimal and temporary.

Paper was the same way. "Where's the letter from Lloyd?" Just the thought was enough to prompt the desire to have the letter there in front of him instantly. It was expected to levitate magically to the top of the pile. And, magically, it often did. I trained myself to remember the arrangement of Jack's desk. If Lloyd's letter was there, I knew precisely where it was and could run in and find it for him (or yell in directions—I, too, did not use the intercom). I was also prompted to try to develop powers of clairvoyance. Often, I would consult my inner oracle to predict what he would ask for and have it near the top of a convenient pile of documents. This really isn't mind reading at all but an awareness of what's on the day's agenda and planning accordingly.

That kind of planning—stacking the document deck—falls under what I call the microplanning category. Instead of thinking of plans in grandiose terms like blueprints and battle plans, scale back to a plan that looks ahead to the next fifteen minutes or half hour. If an item at the top of Jack's agenda involved Lloyd or his operation, I could count on his wanting to see the letter, and I'd make sure it was toward the top of the stack.

I've known since my first day on the job that Jack Welch's boat floats on a sea of questions. By studying the calendar on any given day, I could translate the straightforward list of appointments, meetings, and events outside the office into a tip sheet on the kinds of questions he would want answered over the next eight to ten hours. If he was due to be visited by an important customer, chances were good he would want to know something—make that a lot of things—about the person he would be meeting with, his or her business, and the outstanding issues that prompted the get-together. At least one day before, I would have been in contact with the key GE executives who dealt with that customer to ask for a summary of the relationship, including all the current pluses and minuses. Were there problems? If there were, why? What were we doing to fix them? How long will it take? Was the customer satisfied with our plan? And what was the future state of our relationship likely to be? I knew that the required information was out there in someone's head or file. The challenge was to get it moved into the CEO's office in a usable form.

I'd prepare a one-page synopsis and put it in a folder on Jack's desk. I'd also be prepared to fill him in on whatever details didn't make it into the synopsis. It was often a better use of time—his and mine—to brief him verbally when it became necessary to layer in some details. It was a way to spare me from having to write a multi-page document, and spare him from having to read one.

Since I'm giving away the secrets of my amazing mind-reading act, I should also reveal that I've known for years that my premeeting questions would only scratch the surface. Therefore, I was ready to fire up my Rolodex to call the GE executives he would probably want to talk to personally before or during the meeting. If I could, I made sure I knew their general whereabouts for the day or how we might go about finding them. As a little test of my magic powers, I'd wait at my desk long enough so that I knew he probably had picked up the day's agenda, glanced at the background file, and . . .

"Ro, get me—"

Gary, I'd think as I opened the Rolodex.

"—Gary," he'd finish.

For his part, Gary knew full well who was on the other end when the phone rang, and he also knew that I had asked him all the easy and obvious questions already, and that he was about to see some ninety-eight-mile-per-hour fastballs headed across the plate.

When the light on the phone console went off, I could count to two and . . .

"Ro, get me Beth."

"Beth's out of the country. How about Bruce?" Meanwhile, I'd be dialing Bruce.

"Yeah, Bruce." Although he might just as easily say that he couldn't care less if Beth was out of the solar system, just get her on the phone—in which case I would have told him we'd got an APB out on Beth, and until we found her, Bruce would be a good substitute.

Usually, I kept one ear on the conversation to stay on top of the situation or to be sure I didn't miss a commitment he might make during the conversation. Jack was a serial caller when he phoned in from the road and I was in the office. It made sense for me just to stay on the line and dial into the next call, and the next. As a result, I learned directly from the master just what I should be asking his executives about impending customer visits and many other subjects.

This one technique that I've just mentioned—monitoring phone calls—is worth the price of this book. Being immersed in the substance of the job and keeping up to speed on the events occurring around me was invaluable. Listening in on a variety of incoming and outgoing calls provided a priceless education. Furthermore, by staying on the line I didn't need to be briefed by Jack on a situation or issue. Plus, I knew enough to add the date to the calendar if he made a commitment to travel or attend a meeting. I also could alert him to dates that were already booked and make sure I got a head start on gathering background material and other research information. At times, I would exit an ongoing call to track down supplemental data or answer a pending question, and then I'd come back on the line with an update so that when he hung up he had a more complete picture of the situation.

Does call monitoring inhibit candor? Certainly not internally. I can't think of a single instance where a GE executive was reluctant to speak knowing that I was on the line. In fact, Jack used to feel free to pull me into a conversation by saying things like, "You heard what he said, Ro. Isn't that true?"—as if he needed a witness to verify his story.

Probably the most historic calls I ever monitored came just a few months before Jack retired. You've probably read about GE's ill-fated attempt to acquire Honeywell. I'll discuss the drama surrounding the deal in Chapter 15, but I might as well share the phone monitoring aspect at this point. In the last stages of the proposed Honeywell acquisition, Jack Welch made sure I was on the line when Mario Monti, the European Union's commissioner for competition, called to say that the EU was blocking the acquisition. It was the afternoon of Thursday, June 28. Jack wanted an extra ear since he was going to have to immediately put out a statement to the press and had to make sure we had the legal niceties right. By having me take notes, there was a bit of a safety net in case the lawyers said to him, "Are you sure Monti phrased it that way?" As it was, we were getting one story from Monti's lawyers to our legal team, and another from Honeywell (based on their interpretation of what the EU was saying about its reasons for blocking the merger). I was privy to the Monti/Welch call, the call from Jack to Mike Bonsignore, Honeywell's CEO, and a three-way conversation with Welch, Bonsignore, and Monti. It was an indication of the extra care, caution, and concern that Jack Welch took involving this critical event.

RECORD KEEPING

Why not simply use a tape recorder to preserve these conversations? GE has an informal policy against them, but even so it would be an exercise in sheer drudgery and expense to transcribe and archive millions of hours of calls. Besides, very few notes are worth keeping, including and particularly mine. They are rarely, if ever, looked at a second time. Think about it: How many times have you read through the notes of a meeting you attended three weeks ago? Why do some organizations insist on sending around meeting notes and summaries after a meeting? By the time the material arrives, most participants have moved on to other business.

It varies among individuals, and GE people will take a few notes to help them focus on an action plan once they get out of the meeting, but there's little interest in documentation for the sake of the historical record. I think business enterprises that worry too much about history end up trapping themselves in the past by investing too much time and effort in overarchiving and overanalyzing events that may never repeat themselves. It's a way to create a security blanket, and a false one at that. *Documenting* why you screwed up is no guarantee you won't do it again. If there's a problem, take just enough time to find out what happened, fix it, and move ahead. Business is about today and tomorrow. Chances are that what was important yesterday won't be relevant very far into the future. And if it is, it will make itself felt in the established culture of the organization, not by moldering away in some filing cabinet (or the digital equivalent). I'd say that over fourteen years, there were just a handful of times when Jack Welch needed documents from the files. He preferred to concentrate on current data and future plans.

When he did take notes, it was usually casual and spontaneous. Jack's favorite medium was a scrap of paper or half of a cocktail napkin. For the most part, he was too actively engaged in the real-time give-and-take of a meeting to be able to step back and jot it all down.

About the only conversations that were tape-recorded on occasion were when Jack had contacts with the press and there was a chance he might be misquoted. We'd always let the interviewer know we were taping, of course. It was a purely defensive tactic that made the reporters realize that they might want to take extra care with the accuracy of the story. Every now and then, I would monitor a press call if Jack was concerned that a reporter had a particular ax to grind. I'd listen for the tone and content of the questions. If I heard something that was of concern, we might alert the public relations people that trouble was brewing so they could prepare a response or, more proactively, try to head it off by providing facts and figures that would shoot down a false premise.

SHIPSHAPE

An impatient boss tends to need higher maintenance—Jack Welch did, anyway. The surface of his desk was a work in progress, and a far cry from the Hollywood version of a CEO's fifty square feet of glistening walnut with a surface broken only by a Mont Blanc pen set and a leather-framed photograph of the kids and the golden retriever. To use seagoing analogies, his desk was more like an aircraft carrier than a sleek yacht or a frumpy tugboat. The bow of the USS *Welch* was pointed into the wind, and the vessel was cruising full speed ahead, shipshape and ready to launch its full squadron of attack aircraft.

I was the chief air officer. I'd usually set up the flight deck at night, after he left. It made more sense to organize the desk before I went home rather than face that daunting task in the morning. I didn't want to risk the chance that he'd find a disorganized desk if he got to the office before me. The flight deck had to be ready for immediate launch. The arrangement was carefully orchestrated, so Jack knew he could look for specific categories of material in the same places every day. For visual cues, I color-coded the files: blue for personal, yellow for internal, red for reading, orange for external, and green for signature. Each stack occupied the same bit of territory (until the stack got too high and tipped over).

Jack liked to wrestle with his work, which meant that the folders quickly got spread around. Usually, the contents stayed reasonably close to the folders, but after ten minutes or so I could count on "Ro, where's . . . ?" I'd yell back, "To the left of the phone, the yellow folder, three pages from the top."

As I mentioned earlier, Jack Welch's impatience drove him to practice a form of wishful thinking: *I need a piece of paper, therefore the paper should be found directly beneath my right hand—right now.* I imagine he's been at it since he was six months old and demanding that his mother immediately find the toy that fell through the bars of the crib. The truly remarkable thing is that he has been able to construct an adult lifestyle and workstyle that sees to it that the toy is always there.

When he got up from his desk to go into the adjoining conference room or elsewhere, I would make a foray into the office. I learned not to be too much of a neatnik or he would grumble that I had messed him up by putting away a document that he was still reading. My hit-and-run raids, timed to coincide with his brief absences, were temporary expedients to preserve a modicum of order. When he actually left the office for a longer meeting in another part of the building, I would do a major overhaul and straightening. On those occasions, I would bring in new material and take away the old files that had been worked through. I made a dozen or more housekeeping runs a day.

When Jack was traveling, I would set up his briefcase before the trip to mimic the desktop pattern. The same color-coded folders would go in fixed places so that he would know where to look for what he needed. I'd put the day's calendar in a yellow-tinted plastic cover, and while a document or entire folder might go astray on the road ("Ro, where's . . . ?" "In the red folder." "I left the red folder at home last night."), he carefully guarded the calendar, knowing the consequences if it was lost—although I kept a copy with me twenty-four hours a day, and it was always on my computer.

If these details seem like a load of trivia, I'm laying them out for two reasons. The first is shock value. As much as we lionize some business leaders—a tendency that's subsided somewhat since the collapse of several companies for a variety of reasons related to poor management—the fact is, they need elaborate as well as basic support systems. The second reason is educational value. It's important to know what's required to keep the next level above us functioning productively. The specifics vary from place to place and from person to person, but we need to get over the every-man-for-himself attitude. Nobody can do it alone.

We all need support staff to help us do our own jobs.
No one can do it alone.

One more housekeeping item to demonstrate just how basic the support system can get: wastepaper patrol. When Jack left his desk, I needed to make sure that I knew what he had tossed in the wastebasket. Much of what he looked at—if I was doing my job right—was important enough to probably involve follow-up of some kind. On mail he'd give back, he'd write instructions in the margin or put an executive's initials at the top to indicate how it should be routed. But some stuff was iffy. He might want to see it, he might not. In those cases, if he tossed it in the trash, I would have no idea what had happened to the item. Somebody could be on the phone a week later asking me about it and I wouldn't have an answer. I couldn't just assume it had been tossed; he might have put it aside, or the material might have gotten misplaced.

Jack never liked my wastepaper patrol. When he'd catch me at it, he'd say, "What the hell are you doing? I threw that away!" I think he was afraid that what he had tossed would end up back on his desk and he would waste time reading it again. I kept explaining that I really need to know what he discarded so that we could simply log it—something like "Aruba time-share brochures—discarded by JFW." Then I could tell the persistent real estate salesperson to stop bugging us. Typically, my response would be sugarcoated: "Mr. Welch reviewed your material and has decided against making the investment."

If you have qualms about managing up by going through wastebaskets, that's understandable, and you shouldn't do it. I didn't have those qualms. Everyone has their own threshold and definition of what constitutes indignity. For me, running an operation with knowledge gaps caused by material that comes in and disappears without a trace—that's indignity.

MELLOW YELLOW

A quick word-association game:

Mason's trowel?	Bricklayer.
Hammer?	Carpenter.
Stethoscope?	Doctor.
Tractor?	Farmer.
Yellow highlighter?	Assistant to an impatient boss.

The yellow highlighter was a godsend. It allowed me to radically compress and distill written text quickly and easily. I estimate that something on the order of a half million to a million words a week washed over the CEO's office—thousands of pieces of mail, e-mail, reports, memos, briefing books, Internet material, and various commercial and scholarly publications. Armed with a highlighter, my job was to hack through a wall of words, like a machete through jungle brush.

Jack Welch read fast, skimmed faster, and freely skipped sentences, paragraphs and pages at the first sign of irrelevancy. So did I. Few pieces of paper hit his desk without being worked over by my highlighter. If Jack had tried to read every word, he would have had less time to run GE. I looked for the topic sentence, the main supporting points, and the conclusion. Meanwhile, I was simultaneously on the phone, inputting data into my computer and answering a familiar cry from the next room: "Ro, where's . . . ?" Did things get lost in the process? Probably. But so much of the material that's flung at the average top business executive is totally worthless that the odds of missing anything really important are extremely remote.

It does help to have a sixth sense for the one document that must be read word for word. I didn't have it, but Jack Welch did.

Glancing at my highlights, he could make an instant assessment of whether he had seen enough or should read on. Particularly on internal documents, I'd attach Post-it notes with advisories like "I've alerted Mike about this" or "Checked with Medical Systems and they will get back to you." The Post-its augmented the information or indicated that a follow-up was in the works. Like everything else that went on his desk, I knew the contents of his reading pile, and monitored how fast the pile dwindled. It gave me a sense of whether I was underestimating or overestimating the value of what I was giving him. As the years went by, either he got more impatient or else I got more deadly with the highlighter, because the piles of reading matter tended to disappear a lot faster.

For those who think this system left too much to chance, bear in mind that with GE's talented top executive team behind us, anything that got incorrectly filtered out before reaching Jack or was given short shrift by him would bounce back with another Post-it note attached recommending a rereading.

Skimming, speed reading, and quickly absorbing vast amounts of material depend on the individual, but the one part of our system that would be useful in most other offices is the preprocessing of reading matter. By managing up in this way, you help the person above zero in on the most important elements without acting as a filter. Bosses can stop with the highlights or read as much as they want.

THE PLUSES AND MINUSES

An employee shouldn't try to reinvent his or her manager. I could see a misguided person attempting to change Jack Welch's impatient ways. Lots of luck! Aside from being doomed to failure, the reform effort neglects to take into account that one of the reasons he got the CEO's post and excelled at it was because of his impatience, not in spite of it. He set a blistering pace, slashed away at the bureau-cracy, and drove change relentlessly in an era that was unforgiving of the slow and lumbering cultures of manufacturing behemoths like GE. I suspect that former CEO Reg Jones, who picked Jack to be his successor, did so knowing that Jack's impatience would turn out to be a great asset.

A case could be made that the initial decision to acquire the investment house Kidder, Peabody in 1986 reflected the downside of Jack Welch's impatience with overanalysis and that a more delib-erate approach would have revealed that Kidder wasn't a good fit. But in his memoir, Jack described the decision as a classic case of hubris, commenting, "I was just full of myself." He said he pushed the acquisition because at the time he felt he could make anything work. As someone who's on the side of those who are impatient with overanalysis, inertia, and inaction, I lean more toward impa-tience than hubris as an explanation, although the two characteris-tics may be intertwined. I've learned that if you spend too much time worrying about making mistakes, you never make history. Jack didn't worry about mistakes. But he wasn't just rolling the dice. At the time, the Kidder deal made sense since it allowed GE Capital to save on brokerage fees by working through Kidder and to have bet-ter access to leveraged-buyout opportunities, which in that era were the rage on Wall Street.[1]

I'm not interested in second-guessing the Kidder acquisition; my point relates to what I said about not reinventing your boss. Jack's impatience may have had a downside, but I think it's more useful to stay focused on the upside if you want to manage up effec-tively. The very trait you try to change may be the one that gives that person a special advantage. In an ideal world, all parties compro-mise and make an effort to meet in the middle, but when it comes to managing up, it's always going to be your job to be flexible.

One of the virtues of working for a large business organiza-tion is that the diversity of personal styles and backgrounds creates a unique blend. Cookie-cutter operations—the long line of gray flannel suits, white shirts, and black wing-tip shoes—are dead or dying these days because they can't dip into a bubbling melting pot of talent, personality types, and social backgrounds in response to a bubbling melting pot of a marketplace. Jack Welch was impatient, and many of those who worked closely with him picked up that trait—much to the dismay of some of their assistants— but he tolerated and encouraged other styles and ways of doing business.

———

I'd say there are at least eight huge advantages to cultivating your impatience:

- It leads to rapid response and turnaround.
- Your eyes are on the horizon (the future).
- Time is used more productively.
- It fosters change.
- The focus is on essentials.
- There's less paper.
- Risk taking isn't as daunting.
- You won't be bored.

In his poem "Fire and Ice," Robert Frost considered the two sides of humankind's dilemma—whether to obey the heart or the head. Frost concluded that he would "hold with those who favor fire."[2] But he admitted that ice also had its uses. Similarly, I can weigh the pluses and minuses of patience against impatience and give patience its due. Patience keeps you in the game for the long haul. Patience is a sobering and steadying influence. Cultivating both traits and finding your own balance between them is a good idea. A little fire, a little ice. Personally, though, I hold with those who favor impatience.

Impatience Takeaways

- To work for an impatient boss, you have to be a microplanner.
- Be nosy, but in a good way. Know the who, what, when, where, and how about everything going on in your job.
- Anticipate. I'll say it again: Anticipate.
- Plan for the next day the night before.
- Impatience is a virtue—look where it got Jack Welch!

CHAPTER 5

Energy

TRANQUIL. That's the word that comes to mind first when I set out to describe GE's home office in Fairfield, Connecticut. A couple of low-rise modern office buildings surrounded by trees and mani- cured lawns. Tasteful, restrained, and serious. In many ways the complex epitomizes management guru Peter Drucker's contention that the hallmark of a well-run factory is the lack of noise. In his classic book *The Effective Executive,* Drucker said he learned early in his career as a consultant that a boring factory is a well-run factory. Drama and excitement are signs of poor management.[1]

By that standard, although Fairfield is hardly a factory, the low- key atmosphere at GE's headquarters is clearly in keeping with its status as one of the world's most successful companies. The visitor who checks in at the security gatehouse, parks his car, and strolls past the flower beds into the entrance of the main building can't help but feel calm and reassured. It's not a ghost town by any means, however. There's plenty of genteel hustle and bustle, phones ringing in the distance, people coming and going. Work is being done, but done with dignity and professional decorum. Taking the elevator to the third floor, the visitor emerges into a muted world of thick beige carpeting, walls painted in soothing earth tones and decorated with pastoral oil paintings by famous artists. These days he could saunter the length of the corridor and encounter nary a discordant sound or raised voice.

I say "these days" because just a few years ago he would have been at serious risk of encountering GE's equivalent of Mick Jagger bearing down on him in full cry. The Drucker rule went out the window when Jack Welch was present in this GE "factory." After he retired in September 2001, my colleagues on the third floor, where our office was located, commented that things just weren't the same. They weren't criticizing Jeff Immelt, the new CEO; they were commenting on the sudden lack of noise and drama that had often accompanied a simple Jack Welch journey either into or out of the building.

These sojourns, especially the departures, featured Jack bellowing last-minute instructions: "Ro, don't forget to . . . ," "Ro, make sure you . . . ," and "Ro, did you put the . . . ?" I could hear him without leaving my desk, even though by then he was already half a city block away. Eventually I would have to place a call to my colleagues with offices closer to the elevators, asking, "What did he say?"

The commotion continued the length of the hallway, for the duration of the wait for the elevator to arrive, and often was cut short only by the doors closing in the middle of his sentence: "Ro, don't forget—" And then there was silence (perhaps broken by a muffled ". . . to send a copy . . ." from behind the elevator doors).

Noise was a by-product of Jack Welch's high-energy management style. He wasn't shy about greeting his friends and coworkers, offering praise, leveling criticism, giving orders, and asking questions—often, it seemed, in the same breath. The noise functioned as a stimulant to everyone Jack came in contact with, and as a way to blast away the staid GE placidity that in its worst form could degenerate into passivity and narcolepsy. Nobody was going to go to sleep on Jack Welch's watch. Not a chance.

GOAL TENDING

Working for a high-energy boss is a challenge, especially when he or she routinely puts out 150 percent and expects you to do the same. On paper and in theory, it may not be very appealing to many people who'd prefer to work at a slower, "more reasonable" pace. But I discovered that I liked the speed, the exhilaration, and, yes, even the pressure. If nothing else, such intensity and high energy are antidotes to doing the same old things in the same old ways. It offers a way to stay sharp, stay focused, and stay alive. You hardly notice the hours passing by. The Energizer Bunny doesn't wear a watch.

Jack's pace was so fast it didn't leave time for second-guessing myself or feeling put upon. Does an ice hockey goalie stand there and say, "Gee, I don't know about this"? No, he's too busy for that. He stops the puck, keeps stopping it, and is totally absorbed by what he's doing and loves every hectic second of it. Sports is a good analogy. One of Jack's favorite observations was that business is a game. Seeing your job in this light—particularly if you work long hours under high pressure—can help make it easier. For one thing, people often take their work too seriously. When the going gets heavy, the idea of actually cracking a smile seems sacrilegious. And then there's the fear that starts to well up: fear of failure, fear of mistakes, and fear of the future. It robs us of perspective. Without perspective—the ability to step back and see where we are and where we're headed—we literally lose our bearings; there's no way to tell left from right, up from down, and forward from back. Treating work as a game can restore perspective. We all know how to play a game—keep score, do our best to win, play fair and by the rules, and enjoy yourself.

In a game, it's assumed that sometimes you win and sometimes you lose. It's not a sin to lighten up (see Chapter 7 on humor) and accept that today "the bear ate you," and tomorrow "you'll eat the bear." Life—a high-energy life—will go on even if the deadline is missed, the sale is lost, and the promotion doesn't come through. *Hey, it's only a game!* Not that you don't play energetically and hate to lose. In that regard, one of my most vivid recollections is drawn from one of our darker days—April 14, 1994, when the Kidder, Peabody phantom bond trading scam broke. I mentioned Kidder in the last chapter as a Jack Welch acquisition that might not have been made were it not for his impatience. Maybe, maybe not. I could argue that had Jack really been impatient, he might have dumped Kidder back in 1987 right after Kidder's hotshot investment banker Marty Siegel was caught selling insider stock tips to Ivan Boesky. If he had washed his hands of Kidder then, instead of *patiently* trying to salvage GE's investment in the firm, he would have spared himself from another clobbering.

April 14 was a Thursday, Jack was planning to slip out of town for a long weekend, and we were crazed trying to get things cleaned up before he left.

I had succeeded in fending off most of the last-minute calls and was trying to raise the drawbridge to keep new issues from delaying Jack's departure when Mike Carpenter, Kidder's president, called. Mike was a great guy who had volunteered after the insider trading fiasco to move from a fast-track position at GE Capital to run

Kidder. By the time Mike called, the bridge was almost all the way up. So I said, "Mike, he's trying to leave town, and he's running really late. Can it wait until Monday?"

The formula had worked so many times before, I wasn't ready for his answer. "No, I'm afraid it can't."

If he had said, "Put him on, because there may not be a Monday," it would have had about the same shock value. Without getting an explanation of the crisis from Mike, I knew from his voice that the situation was serious. As it turned out, there was no long weekend—not in the mini-vacation sense, anyway. Jack took the phone call. Soon after, there were changes in a lot of people's weekend plans.

Carpenter's call was to inform the CEO that the head of Kidder's government bond desk was suspected of faking trades to inflate his annual bonus, and that to square the books, Kidder would need to take a $350 million write-off against first-quarter earnings. Some game, eh? We lost a round, but like a game it wasn't over until it was over.

What we had all been looking forward to as a quickie spring break turned into a hectic blur of telephone calls as Jack Welch scrambled to assess the damage. And as a postscript to the patience-impatience theme of the last chapter, six months later, in October of 1994, GE sold Kidder to PaineWebber for $670 million and a 24 percent equity position in PaineWebber, which netted another $2 billion when PaineWebber was eventually bought out. *Now* the game was over.

LATE NIGHTS, LONG HOURS

A drawback of working for a golfer is that most clubs ban cell phones from the course, which means that a key executive is out of touch for a couple of hours. Now, that wasn't a great hardship for

Jack Welch since he never carried a cell phone anyway. And I guess I should digress a little and explain why.

He would have been the Johnny Appleseed of cell phones by leaving them everywhere. As I recall, we got him one when they first came out, and it lasted a couple of days before it vanished without a trace. It wasn't that he was forgetful or absentminded; he just had better things to do than pick up his cell phone. Secondly, Jack had easy access to more phones than most human beings own over the course of a lifetime. All of the cars he rode in had phones; so did the helicopters and the corporate jets. I am surprised the phone company didn't assign him his own private area code. As you read the story that opens this chapter—the visitor to Fairfield encountering GE's Mick Jagger—you might have wondered why I didn't just walk him to the elevators instead of listening to him yell instructions. Now you know: I might not have made it back to my desk in time to catch his first call. As soon as he hit the car waiting for him outside the lobby door, he would grab the phone and dial me. It was the same for the handoff from the car to the chopper, the chopper to the jet, the jet back to the car, and onward to his destination. The phone was in almost constant use and all the calls went straight through our office.

Over the course of a typical year, I probably had only a few weekends that were not broken up by phone calls or work-related activities. Seeing that in print makes me extremely queasy. I don't want to create the impression that I worked for a slave driver. The hours were largely self-inflicted. Frankly, I have to say that I like to work—and I particularly enjoyed the excitement and challenges of working at such a senior level. The long hours and the intense demands of the job didn't bother me much at all. And I must add that these long hours and intense involvement produced a handsome income and lifestyle for which I am grateful.

I'll give you a non–Jack Welch example to demonstrate how incorrigible I really am. Because NBC owned the broadcast rights, and GE owned NBC, we had a major company presence at the 1996 Olympics, which were in Atlanta, Georgia. I was on the corporate team—just to distinguish the real athletes from the rest of us—that handled the logistical arrangements on the ground in Atlanta for GE's board of directors, senior executives, and other guests. After running around all day in the heat, troubleshooting, straightening out snafus, and whatnot, the team would routinely hold meetings at midnight to strategize and plan for the next day. The sessions would last until two or three o'clock in the morning, and we had to be out of bed by five. Grueling? A pain in the neck? A major imposition?

I loved it, including the crazy hours and the meals on the run! The laughs, creative problem solving, and interaction with my teammates made the time whip by. We didn't conquer the world, make a lot of money, sign a big deal, or win a gold medal. The mission was to get members of the GE family to and from the Olympic events. Not the stuff of an MBA thesis, but we did it well and had a great time.

This story, with all of its lack of a jazzy punch line, may tell you more about me than the stories that you'll read in the pages ahead. I didn't need Jack Welch or the prestige of the CEO's office to provide a buzz. I got it from interaction with the team, the sense of shared purpose, and accomplishing a mission. My energy source isn't a desk or a telephone, it's other people. That's why I went to work early and came home late. I'll discuss the importance of teamwork later in the book, but for now it's enough to say that for me working in isolation is an energy spoiler. Put me on a team, let us loose, and the long hours mean nothing. The team can be two people or two hundred.

Interacting with a team, with a sense of shared purpose, is an incredible high.

And I need to correct something I wrote earlier. I said I like to work. I don't, really. I love to play; it just happens that for me it's called work. If managing up effectively is your goal, you'll need to form a team with the person above, join that team wholeheartedly, and play on! While no one should expect to have to put in the kind of hours that I did, you do need to give it 110 percent, to be committed to getting the job done, no matter what it takes.

**Be committed to getting the job done—
no matter what it takes.**

THE ULTIMATE ROAD WARRIOR

Jack was out of the office and on the road an average of three or four days a week. The road trips were his way of staying in close touch with the diverse and far-flung GE empire. What's wrong with the telephone? you might legitimately ask. Or was the e-mail system down? The answer is that in terms of energy, the phone and e-mail take a backseat to face-to-face, person-to-person encounters.

I just said that my energy source is people. Well, you can square that, cube it, in applying it to Jack Welch. He said many times that GE is in the business of making great people who turn around and make great products and services. In his memoirs, he dubbed GE the "people factory." And here again, with apologies to Peter Drucker, it was a *noisy* factory indeed. Jack hardly needed an excuse to pack his bags and climb on the company plane. When he hit a town—Cleveland, Atlanta, Paris, wherever—questions flew fast and furious. I recall one poor driver who met us at the airport in Louisville being battered by dozens of questions ranging from the weather forecast, the traffic patterns, and the local sports teams to where the man had gone to school. It was a preview of the kind of run-and-gun interrogation that Jack would always employ to both find out what our business leaders were doing with their time and resources and drive the energy levels sky-high. There's nothing quite like having your CEO spraying you with questions to get the adrenaline flowing.[2]

I'm convinced that while many visiting senior executives don't mind and even expect to generate a little awe and admiration, Jack Welch couldn't have given two twits about that. He intended to create buzz and excitement that would linger on after he had departed. Energy begets energy. In that sense, a high-energy leader is using energy (his) to create more energy (theirs). There's an element of role modeling involved as well. Jack was giving his subordinates a lesson on how to go about running a high-energy business. He wanted them to learn to ask questions—lots of them—and listen closely to the answers. Jack wasn't trying to put people on the spot with his questions. He sought information directly from those who were on the firing line, knowing there's no better place for an executive to educate himself. And if someone fumbled or didn't seem to be in command of facts that she should have been conversant with given her position, Jack wanted to know that, too.

The role modeling extended down the leadership hierarchy to all employees. As often as he could, Jack would combine a budget review or strategy session conducted at one of the operating units with a facility tour. It gave him a chance to publicly demonstrate with deeds, not just words, some of the policies he had been advocating for so many years. One of his favorite moves was to break away from the formal guided tour of the plant and single out a timid-looking worker to ask him some general questions, such as what he did and how long he had worked there. The Welch style and chemistry are such that the ice usually melts immediately. Blue-collar guys love to talk to him, perhaps sensing his salt-of-the-earth origins. Often, a worker steeped in the "boundaryless" culture of GE and recalling the lingering vestiges of the Work-Out era would bring up a problem that he had been having. Jack listened closely but always replied, "What have you done to solve the problem?"

He wanted to drive home the message that it was up to individuals to solve their problem, not senior management. Sure, Jack was in charge, but what he wanted was for the people on the front lines, the ones who knew what needed to be done, to step in and find a solution instead of relying on top management to come up with one that might not be as savvy as it would be if it came from the people who have seen the problem up close.

Individuals solve problems—not senior management.

Whenever he turned the tables like that and asked what the worker had done about the issue, you could almost see a light bulb go on as the guy said to himself, *Me? Well, I guess I could talk to . . .*

By then—and the incident that I'm recalling here probably occurred in 1998 or 1999—the theme of idea sharing had been so embedded into the new GE, thanks to tireless Jack Welch preaching, that the worker stood a pretty good chance of being listened to and having her ideas seriously considered. Idea sharing was such gospel that you could end up getting fired for *not* sharing ideas or for discouraging others' ideas. Talk about changes. In 1980, soon after I had joined GE, I went to an executive to point out the wastefulness of allowing each division to buy incompatible technology (as discussed a bit in Chapter 2). People were forever grousing that one piece of Fairfield hardware or software wouldn't work with what Cleveland or Louisville was using. Our department manager gave me a cold stare and said, "Go back to your desk." He didn't want to hear about it. Today, he'd listen and probably take my complaint seriously. In the new GE he wouldn't be able to keep me quiet until I got a satisfactory answer. People don't go back to their desks quietly anymore. They don't stand for management's dismissing their legitimate suggestions.

A guaranteed way to short-circuit your success at managing up is to attempt to block the flow of ideas from the individuals below to the person above. Let 'em rip: suggestions, complaints (always accompanied by a proposed solution), good news and bad. Real-world ideas and information are precious commodities. Turn yourself into a pipeline and feed the boss what he or she needs to know.

THE STAY-AT-HOME

It wasn't until our last couple of years that I started traveling occasionally with Jack on domestic trips. Until then, we had assumed that I needed to stay behind to hold down the fort. But after I made my first foreign trip with him to Paris in 1997, due to the illness of the person who normally handled international travel planning, it dawned on us that it was very useful to have me on the scene. "I don't know why I didn't bring you with me years ago" was his reaction. What the change meant from a practical standpoint for me was that some of the forward-looking work, such as meeting planning and the research that it involved, had to be put aside for my return. The trade-off was that my presence allowed Jack to function in real time as though he were back in the home office. He didn't travel with a computer, but I did, which allowed us to stay on top of e-mail as well as access everything the Internet had to offer. We had documents at our fingertips to augment the research that had been done for the trip's scheduled meetings. By my accompanying him, we also eliminated the backlog of material that tended to accumulate in Jack's absence, and cut down on the frenzy that was required to clear his desk when he got back home.

The travel was fascinating and educational, but frankly it added considerably to my workload and in some cases was an inefficient use of my time. A day or two on the road meant that I was that much further behind on some of the projects I had waiting for me back home. The "next" things didn't stop coming because I was out of the office. As a result, we were selective about what trips I went on, tending to favor the ones of longer duration or those to countries with more challenging communications. Even so, I think it's important to try to gain a direct working knowledge of the territory, the issues, and the personalities whenever feasible.

On one trip with Jack, I toured a GE Power Systems turbine manufacturing plant in Greenville, South Carolina. Before that experience, I practically couldn't have told you the difference between a turban and turbine, and while my lack of expertise probably wasn't noticeable in the way I had been dealing with GE Power Systems to that point, at least I gained a visual sense of what went on in the factory and a deeper appreciation for how sophisticated the manufacturing process was. Also, by visiting their home turf, it helped me to deepen my working relationship with key Power Systems people.

Whether to travel or not to travel was always a judgment call. If I stayed back at the home office in Fairfield, I could still be effective as a facilitator and troubleshooter. I sent Jack out with a bare-bones agenda for each day, mainly a list of times, places, names, and coded entries to indicate the purpose of each meeting or event—nothing elaborate, one page per day. I've seen agendas that were works of art, but I didn't have time for art. Into his scruffy old briefcase went background folders for each event. I kept a duplicate, as well as folders packed with nitty-gritty logistical details that I had gathered in the course of research prior to the trip, including the names of people I could call to fix things if there was a problem. For instance, if a car didn't show up at the airport to meet Jack's plane and he called in to ask me if he was supposed to walk into town from the airport, I could get on the phone to the limo dispatcher and straighten things out (a car at the right airport but the wrong terminal was known to happen). Meanwhile, I was free to do other things in between those troubleshooting phone calls, which kept me from falling behind in making arrangements for the next week's or next month's agenda.

When Jack was on the road, my hours were, if anything, longer, particularly on the back end of the day. He is both an early bird and a night owl, and that's why he was hard to keep up with (I myself am just a night owl). The good thing was that he was not a fan of early breakfast meetings. He'd do them when he had to—for example, if an important customer wanted one—but at least once a week or more I had to discourage hard-charging executives from setting up "sunrise services" to prove to Jack how high-energy they were. Our standard start time for events at corporate headquarters was 8:30 A.M. I think he felt that most people needed a little time in the morning to get organized, set their day in motion, or deal with pending issues. However, on the road or at home, he wasn't averse to dinner meetings that would stretch late into the evenings, which meant I could count on getting a call from him immediately afterward to get the ball rolling on whatever business he'd just been discussing.

HIGH-ENERGY QUESTION, HIGH-ENERGY ANSWER

Late calls notwithstanding, I never for a moment grumbled at Jack Welch's extensive travel. A stay-at-home CEO would have made my life a lot easier, but Jack fed off people, not papers, and was drawn irresistibly to that source of energy. Knowing that, it was easy for me to crank up my own energy level to deal with important work that was central to his mission. To have an effective partnership with your boss, you have to adopt the boss's causes as your own. I liked the idea of helping to run a people factory and was willing to bust butt so that Jack and I could form a great partnership. Here's a simple question: Do you know what your boss's goals are?

Think about it. If you have trouble answering the question, there's a problem. The person above you has goals—I guarantee it! They shape his or her behavior in fundamental ways. Knowing what those goals are amounts to having a road map. It won't show every turn or pothole, but you'll have a rough idea of where your manager is headed and what will be required of you. And presumably you too have goals. Are they aligned and compatible with those of the person above?

Being trapped for fourteen years in a "people factory" would have been sheer hell if I hadn't shared Jack's passion for helping people grow and be successful. No amount of money or prestige would have made it bearable.

You need to do a goal check. If your goals mesh with your manager's, stand by for fission, fusion, and a blast of high energy.

If not, it may explain why your energy levels are low these days.

Energy Takeaways

- Beware the too-quiet office. It may be a sign that energy and enthusiasm have bottomed out.
- Business is a game—keep score, try to win, play fair, and have fun. Be committed to get the job done—no matter what it takes.
- If you feel time drags at the office, you need a new job.
- Senior management doesn't solve problems—individuals do.
- Bring passion and commitment to your work. Otherwise, it's not worth doing.

CHAPTER 6

Resilience

I DON'T RECALL having one as a child, but you might have been the proud owner of an inflatable punching bag, wide at the bottom, narrow at the top, with the image of a clown painted on it and a load of sand in its base for ballast. Give it a smack. Over it went. Bong! Back it sprang. Whap! Bong! Whap! Bong! In a simple way, that toy epitomized resilience. Knock it over and back it came.

In a business environment, the punching bag can serve as a useful model. But instead of a load of sand in the base to act as a counterbalance, what's needed is a set of resilience-forming habits. Foremost among them is the certain knowledge that whatever problem occurs, it cannot and will not be allowed to undermine the integrity of the organization.

In the thirteen years I worked in the CEO's office at GE, I saw a number of crises come and go. Each one was very different in terms of the issues, the businesses involved, and the people whose lives were affected. But each was handled with the exact same attention to protecting GE's values and principles. The last thing I want to do in this chapter is reprise every bad patch we encountered, but one in particular comes to mind that proves my point.

On November 17, 1992, NBC's prime-time news program, *Dateline*, broadcasted a fifty-seven-second clip of videotape purporting to show how the gas tanks of certain late-model GM pickup trucks were vulnerable to exploding and burning in side-impact collisions. What the tape did not show was that individuals retained by *Dateline* had attached incendiary devices under the test vehicles, and they were detonated remotely to cause ignition just before the truck was hit.

Three months later, General Motors announced that it would sue NBC for allegedly rigging the trucks in the crashes. The next day, the network apologized on the air for the incident. And what a day it was. From early in the morning to seconds before Jane Pauley went on live to read the apology, our office was throbbing with activity. As NBC's parent company, GE's legal department and senior management were in the thick of things all day. The phones rang nonstop, and there was a series of concerned executives parading through our conference room for hours.

Let me point out before I go any further that this is not an official account but a personal recollection, so I am not in a position to say who decided what and when. But at some point in the process, it was clear that a delay in action was not an option. An apology was due and was going to be delivered immediately. True to Parkinson's law—*work expands to fit the time available*—the wording of the statement to be read by *Dateline* anchor Jane Pauley bounced back and forth among the lawyers and senior executives up to and past the show's 9 P.M. airtime.

I believe that the speed and determination exhibited by everyone involved to put the issue to rest was a product of the GE culture of integrity. When one of your businesses is facing an issue as serious as this, you tend not to throw caution to the wind. Everything becomes very studied and very deliberate. At some companies, though, decision making and dithering could stretch into months or years. Yet there we were, one day later, racing along at full speed with the sole intent of resolving the dispute and doing what was right. This integrity is a key ingredient in creating the resilience habits that I mentioned at the beginning of the chapter. We took a punch and bounced back immediately without having to ponder a response. From there, we moved on.

The language of the apology was still being drafted and typed—and redrafted and retyped—as the show approached the last live segment. Miss the window, miss the opportunity. As I moved back and forth between my desk and the bustling conference room, I kept waiting to hear somebody suggest that we call a time-out. What I heard instead was question after question from Jack being directed at the lawyers and addressed to the others in the room. There wasn't a hint of hesitation. The problem was going to be fixed that night.

After about the tenth revision, I yanked the final statement out of the printer as soon as it cleared and fed it into the fax, took a deep breath, and carefully punched in the fax number in the *Dateline* studio. It rang once and was on its way. We were trying to beat the clock—a live clock—and I prayed we wouldn't experience a mechanical failure. (This was before the days of e-mail.)

Man, did that transmission seem slow! A watched teakettle has nothing on a watched fax machine. It probably didn't take more than fifteen seconds, but I had more than enough time to look at the fax, check the TV to see how the segments were running, and get back to the fax. Finally, the sheet cleared and the transmission concluded.

Now all eyes in the office were glued to the TV. Was there even time to get the text into the Teleprompter? The live segment came up; Jane Pauley looked straight into the camera and read the apology on behalf of NBC.

Subsequently, there was a shakeup at NBC News, including the resignations of Michael Gartner, its president, and of *Dateline*'s executive producer.

A lesser organization would have circled the wagons until the controversy blew over or quietly arranged a settlement with GM. As it was, NBC was mightily embarrassed and horrified that the event had been able to occur and go that far without being detected or reported. There was talk that the news division's reputation had been compromised to the point that it would never recover. Yet today, as I write this, NBC's *Nightly News* is the number-one-rated network newscast. By sticking to their principles of fairness and responsibility, GE and NBC had the resilience to weather the storm.

TOMORROW AND TOMORROW

The next day, after the adrenaline high of the night before, was an anticlimax. But they always were. A sure sign of a resilient operation is that it moves on after the previous day's near-death experience.

Jack Welch tended to turn the page immediately in just about everything he did. His only interest was in what the future held. A couple of times I asked him how a meeting or a special event had gone the night before, particularly if I'd had to jump through hoops to make it happen. He would look at me like he didn't have the slightest idea what I was talking about.

"Last night, the dinner at . . . ?" I'd prompt.

"Oh, fine. It was great." He wasn't interested in reviewing past history. It was over. Even major business meetings that had been carefully prepped, and which anywhere else would have been the subject of morning-after postmortems, got a "Good. No problem." Onward!

Keeping a fast pace was an important element in Jack's leadership style. Dwelling in the past, even if it was only yesterday or an hour before, slowed things down. But I don't think this was at all calculated. What was done was done, as far as he was concerned. *Now let's focus on something else* was his attitude.

That's not to say there wasn't appropriate follow-through. In the case of NBC, Jack took a direct role in recruiting Andy Lack as the news division's new president. This amounted to yet another resilience marker: When there is trouble and personnel shifts must occur, use it as an opportunity to strengthen your team instead of licking your wounds and bemoaning your losses. Hiring Lack—and Jack always insisted on interviewing the finalist and signing off on the decision before an executive at that level came aboard—led to NBC News's comeback. So you could say that without the GM truck fiasco, there might not have been a rejuvenated news division.

Transforming mistakes into opportunities is the hallmark of a resilient organization.

Turn mistakes into opportunities.

THE OTHER KIND OF EXECUTION

You'd have to ask Andy Lack to rate the hiring experience à la Welch from his perspective, but Jack described it in his book by saying that Lack "charmed the hell out of me." As for being fired by Jack Welch, I've witnessed it several times and can say that if one's employment has to be terminated, there are worse ways of getting the ax. He hated doing it but refused to pass the buck. Anyone who reported into the corporate executive office got the news directly from the CEO. On those days, his good humor was practically nonexistent. Sue Baye and I referred to them as "raw meat days," as in carefully slide open the door to his office, toss in the raw meat (actually, quietly drop the day's mail on the desk), and run for it before we got snapped at. He'd work himself into a terribly irritable mood, anticipating what he was going to have to do later in the day. He always admitted it was the part of his job he hated the most and agonized over it until the deed was done.[1]

Ironically, though, many of the people who were about to be sacked didn't go out kicking and screaming. For one thing, most of them knew long before that things weren't working out. Jack never hid bad news or sugarcoated it. If you weren't cutting it, he told you in no uncertain terms long before it got anywhere near being a farewell meeting. He wasn't torturing a hapless victim; he was giving a valued team member an opportunity to correct his or her problems. The strategic planning process in an operation like GE is such that the goals for each business are carefully spelled out. In effect, top management makes the commitment to what it takes to achieve their objectives, and it's perfectly clear to everyone involved what the consequences are if the commitment to share in the company's values isn't maintained. Resilient business organizations and resilient people know where they stand. Those who had goals beyond what was expected of them and had fallen short were never punished.

Before things got to the endgame stage, there would have been ample warning, possibly including an invitation to take as much time as needed to find a suitable position elsewhere. Jack always believed that it doesn't do anybody a favor—the employee or GE's shareholders—to keep a person in a job that's not right for him or her. It's misguided kindness that boomerangs back as cruelty—cruelty for carrying someone for five years, from, say, his mid-forties into his fifties, when he could have and should have been cut loose at an age when he might have landed a good, more suitable job in his prime years. Not to mention the damage done to the organization when the wrong person is in the wrong position.

His view was that while the individual wasn't right for GE in these particular circumstances, there was another job out there that could make the most of that person's unique combination of talents. As a result, what could have had the grimness of an execution frequently took on the air of a career-counseling session and, most notably, a friendly exchange of good wishes. Another factor that militated against angry scenes was that GE offered terrific placement services and generous severance packages.

But the prevailing attitude from executives asked to leave the company was often one of relief. A high-level corporate job, particularly one that's going badly, is no picnic. It's a heavy burden with months, sometimes years of grueling stress and personal sacrifice. I sensed that many of those who came for a last visit with Jack Welch looked upon it as the first day of the rest of their lives, a chance to start over.

CONTROL

It's possible to train yourself to be resilient—sort of like mastering the art of fire walking. A lot of it has to do with attitude. When something goes wrong, I tell myself that whatever happens, while it may be inconvenient, uncomfortable, and an out-and-out pain in the butt, it's no big deal in the vast scheme of things. I have comforted myself during many a bad week with the certain knowledge that Friday would eventually arrive and that next Monday I stood a chance of getting things off to a better start.

One of my pet peeves, which was put on earth to make me strong and resilient, was (and still is) Jack Welch's habit of making last-minute changes in arrangements that had been made, with his approval, weeks in advance and which had consumed hours of time to set up. To become resilient on this issue, I first had to psychoanalyze his behavior. Unlike impatience, which I blamed on his mother, this one is all about control. If you recall, in Chapter 1, I related the story of my job interviews with Jack Welch. What I didn't include—because I wanted to save it for this chapter—was that we did have a short discussion of his concern about his assistant's managing his daily business. Basically, he didn't want an assistant who would try to run his life. Fair enough. At the time, I assured him I was interested not in running his life but rather in supporting him to the best of my ability. The way he chose to run his life was *his* business.

Spin forward to the bane of my existence: the official calendar. From aircraft and air crew availability to juggling the finely calibrated schedules of the people Jack met with, there were dozens of pieces to fit together. If one of those pieces was changed, all of them were affected. It wasn't the act of making the changes that bothered me, it was the waste of time.

Almost every week for fourteen years, I could count on having Jack look at the current calendar—the one in play that week or even that very day—and make changes. He'd announce that he would not depart the night before, as scheduled, but the next morning (or some such variation), thereby blowing out the early morning meetings and setting off a mad scramble for transportation. Could his decision have been made at about the time I'd originally cleared the arrangements with him? With the exception of last-minute emergencies and unanticipated developments, yes. I used to hyperventilate about it, but in time learned to be resilient and chalk it up to his need for control. Also, I came to realize that his sense of time is such that anything beyond the range of a day or two ahead amounted to the distant future. He lives in the present. Asking for approval weeks in advance was necessary for me but not for him. He just wouldn't focus that far out and, therefore, gave me what amounted to a tentative or provisional okay. When the event came within range of the present—sometimes on the very brink of it—I got the answer to my questions.

Did figuring out Jack's thought processes make my life any easier? No. I still had to go through the motions of setting up the schedule in advance, if for no other reason than some of the other people involved couldn't operate any other way. If I was lucky, I could salvage 60 or 70 percent of the schedule. It taught me how to be a skilled maker of excuses. Internally, I could just say to GE people, "We're going to have to change this," without an explanation. I got so that I could easily detect the gnashing of teeth or faint whimpering on the other end of the phone line, and I always felt bad about it.

The GE ground transportation team handled those last-minute changes with composure. John Sullivan, who ran the department, was the complete can-do guy. He proved that to all of us at the 1996 summer Olympics in Atlanta, when Jack suddenly countermanded a decision that had been in place for weeks to bus GE board members and other distinguished guests from event to event. Using limousines was out of the question. It wasn't as if our VIPs had never been on buses before. But Jack wanted vans instead of buses, and he came up with the idea on the morning of the group's arrival, when every van north of Key West and south of Richmond was spoken for. Sullivan was a total gentleman when he got the change in plans, even though he had every right to explode, and a few hours later we had vans. He should write his own book about how he pulled it off. It wouldn't surprise me to find out that John bought an entire fleet of vans hot off the assembly line in Detroit and had them airlifted in.

Similarly, when the arrangements involved one of our businesses, in a phone call I might preface the news by saying, "Don't have a heart attack, but . . ." The length of the silence on the other end was a reliable gauge as to how serious a disruption it would cause to vacations, soccer games, visits to the dentist, and carefully programmed meetings. I'd soften the blow by saying, "He's got a conflict" or "He just can't get away." Externally to GE, however, sudden changes in plans need to be properly packaged. Usually, I invoked the unexpected-emergency excuse, which tended to work well since there isn't a company that doesn't experience them on a regular basis. Sometimes, I'd suggest that I screwed up.

What? Take the fall for somebody else? If that comes as a shocking notion, you might want to recheck the title on the front cover of the book you are now reading. Managing up may mean taking a hit for the person above you to preserve his or her effectiveness. It would be pointless and destructive to place the blame for the schedule changes back on Jack. I was not above covering for him. It's an important skill. If he wanted to control the situation by making last-minute changes, that was his prerogative. My responsibility was to figure out a way to allow him to do that. One technique was to keep a file with all the contacts and their phone numbers readily available in case I needed to get hold of them at the last minute. As a rule, I am not a pack rat. I live to throw away material that's no longer needed. But I hoard anything and everything that might be useful when it's nine o'clock at night and I'm trying to reach some hapless conference planner to tell her one of her star attractions won't make the midmorning session but will be there for lunch. Those files don't get tossed until after it's all over. *Hoarding* is an ugly term, but the practice is a useful resilience habit.

Another technique was to try to warn the other party that the situation might be subject to change. This wasn't easy, however, since they tended to misread the signals. Did I ever complain to Jack? No, it would have gone in one ear and out the other. But

I have to say that when a customer or a non-GE company was involved, he would back off a last-minute change if it would damage a relationship or cause a problem. In those cases, I would just explain what was involved and he'd go with the original plan.

Being resilient requires flexibility.

Every manager has his or her own style. To manage up effectively, you have to take into consideration the individual's unique combination of personal preferences, strengths, weaknesses, quirks, flourishes, and refinements. Being resilient requires flexibility. You have to bend and stretch to accommodate the person above. Whenever I found myself becoming irritated by Jack's last-minute calendar changes, I'd tell myself to just get over it, which is another way of saying, "Just get resilient."

GOOD OLD MURPHY

We're all familiar with Murphy's law. The exact wording of this law depends on the source, and there isn't a reliable one that I know of. My version is: What can go wrong will go wrong. And I've seen a corollary to Murphy's law attributed to the late Texas senator John G. Tower: What can't go wrong will go wrong. Every human institution, from marriage to armed combat, is subject to being Murphyized. Want to excel at your job and keep your organization going at top speed? Learn to always be on the lookout for Murphy's law and have a well-laid defense in place.

I maintain that success in life—any sort of success—depends on your ability to ride out Murphy's law and still achieve your objectives. A Murphy-free life, let alone a Murphy-free business, is an impossibility.

I don't consider myself a pessimist, but I can't think of a task I didn't perform without first looking over my shoulder for Murphy. It motivated me to take extra steps to make sure I had covered every base and a few extra, yet there were times when I was simply bracing myself for Murphy's "gotcha."

If you're expecting a visit from Murphy, it means that you're ready to go with plan B, C, or D. And who knows—plan B might turn out to be a stroke of genius. At the same time, it is much easier to bounce back when it's not your fault that things have gone badly and blame can be dumped on Murphy's doorstep.

UNDER THE KNIFE

At times, resilience calls for lots of chicken soup and a good physician. For Jack that time came in late April 1995, when he suffered a heart attack and underwent an angioplasty to open his blocked artery a day or so later. Unfortunately, the blood vessel closed shortly after the procedure and triggered a second attack. The doctors opened the vessel again without major surgery, but it was rough going. On the afternoon of these procedures, I relieved his wife at the hospital and had the feeling I wasn't cut out for that kind of duty. I had myself convinced that he was going to take a sudden turn for the worse, and I would be the only one sitting there. I thought, *Just don't die on me!* He woke up and—true to form—wanted me to make a phone call for him. The hospital's phones required a telephone credit card number. *Great*, I thought, *I can't remember that old number we used to use* (I direct-dialed most all of his calls), and he certainly wouldn't be able to remember in his groggy condition. But sure enough, he reeled off a telephone credit card number. I keyed it in dubiously, figuring it had to be wrong. He was right, of course.

On May 12, he had open-heart surgery to perform a bypass and was out of the office for about four weeks. During the first ten days at home, he stayed away from all work-related material and caught up on his sleep, read, and watched TV (when I called every morning, I was appalled to hear Jerry Springer in the background). I started bringing some of the mail by for him to look at, just enough to let him ease back in. There were hundreds of get-well cards and notes. He personally answered most of those, which kept him occupied without trying to tackle GE work too soon. Waves of exhaustion would roll over him suddenly while we worked; he would get a look on his face that said, *Okay, that's enough.* I'd quickly pack up and go back to the office.

When he finally returned to the office a few weeks later, we figured that he'd work half days for quite some time. However, the half days lasted only for three days before he was back at it full time.

As for minding the store in his five-week absence, we went into a mode similar to one that kicked in when Jack was on a long trip. The management team was just that—a team. There were no power plays or attempted palace coups; they divided up the responsibilities and went about smoothly running the company. I would bring important issues that surfaced to the vice chairman or our chief financial officer so they would know what was up. We had periodic brief meetings in the conference room to coordinate, communicate, and make sure nothing slipped through the cracks. Things went so well, you would have thought we had done it many times before.

In a situation like that, continuity is important. Jack's process and priorities remained unchanged. Sudden shifts and new initiatives would have been disruptive. But that didn't mean important work came to a standstill. Pending issues and deals moved through the administrative pipeline without interruption. If anything, we were probably a little more attentive to effective communication to make sure the executive team was fully briefed, yet the Welch signature breakneck pace of doing business hardly slackened at all.

Resilience Takeaways

- If you get knocked down, be prepared to bounce back immediately.
- Treat your mistakes as opportunities for growth.
- What's done is done. Don't dwell on the past. Learn from your mistakes and move on.
- Be flexible. Always have a backup plan, or two . . . or three . . .

CHAPTER 7

Humor

EVER SINCE I BEGAN quoting Peter Drucker, I've been toying with the idea of propounding my own Peter Drucker–like maxims. My favorite is: A lack of laughter is a sign of a business that is in trouble, is headed for trouble, or deserves to be in trouble.

I don't expect to see this gem in *Bartlett's Familiar Quotations* anytime soon, and I realize it will face questions like "What about the funeral business?"

Perhaps I should just fall back on a more cautious proposition: If you've got to go to work every day, laughter makes it easier to bear. A lot easier. In fact, without laughter and a general atmosphere of good humor, I never would have made it to five years at GE, let alone twenty-five. Humor and hard work supplied the glue that kept my working partnership with Jack Welch together and gave it strength.

In researching this book, I was struck by how humor served as a safety valve during some pretty unfunny moments. For example, in the summer of 2001, as Jack was about to retire, the Environmental Protection Agency handed him a major disappointment. The EPA ruled that GE must bear the cost of dredging a fifty-mile stretch of the Hudson River for PCB contamination, regardless of scientific studies that show the pollution levels have been dropping on their own and that the remedy may make the problem worse by stirring up and spreading the PCBs from the river sediment.

Jack had been fighting the dredging scheme ever since it was first proposed by environmental activists and formally put forward by the Clinton administration. Because the PCBs had been released into the river by two GE plants prior to the mid-1970s, the company was willing to pay for an effective cleanup—but not one that, in Jack's opinion, was based on questionable science and partisan politics. While the PCB discharge had not occurred on his watch as CEO, Jack Welch became the target of the environmental groups because he refused to simply write the check and be done with it. He made dozens of speeches and gave countless press interviews on the issue, hoping that the force and logic of his argument would make a difference.

When it didn't, I remember being struck by the temperate reaction within GE to the news. Sure, there was disappointment, and a few four-letter words were uttered. But what really stood out was the comment from a GE executive who had spent years handling the issue. As a conference call linking Jack and his team was concluding, Steve Ramsey, our vice president of environmental programs, said, "I'm going to go down into my basement tonight, search around for the most expensive bottle of wine that I own, and drink every drop of it."

And so the battle ended, not with a bang or a whimper, but with a chuckle. It probably sent a few of us home to ransack our own wine supplies that evening.

COMIC TIMING

One of the jobs I did for Jack Welch was to be a one-woman laugh track. Not that I was yukking it up all the time, but I realized early in my career that somebody needed to lighten things up, otherwise the aura of power that came with the CEO's office would be unbearable. Visitors, particularly first-timers and those who didn't normally move in senior management circles, would arrive for meetings at our office nearly paralyzed with fear. One of my favorite tricks was to say, "Mr. Mathews, it's so nice to see you," pausing to let the man gasp for air between his clenched teeth, his eyes as wide as the proverbial deer in the headlights, "but we were expecting you tomorrow. Mr. Welch is not here today." My comic timing is pretty good. I'd wait as his face started to turn crimson, then toss in, "Just kidding. He's down the hall; be back in a minute."

As you're reading this, that may seem cruel. But the jolt snapped some people out of the trance they had put themselves in and reminded them that they were not going to the guillotine but coming for a meeting with a reasonably normal guy. (*Reasonably* is all I'm committing to.)

I think Sue Baye, who was my administrative partner in our office, expected my joke to send somebody into cardiac arrest one day. I'm convinced, however, that the laughter it drew from visitors—and they always laughed from relief that they hadn't screwed up the date—jump-started normal respiration and *prevented* heart attacks.

Even so, I probably did cause a few ulcers with a standard joke I pulled to tease overly aggressive GE colleagues who bombarded me with e-mail in their eagerness to win Jack's approval for a special project or to get his feedback. The wording of the messages varied but usually featured a question like "Can you give me any indication as to when Mr. Welch will respond to this matter?" After two or three of these missives, I would strike back by forwarding the query to Jack's e-mail box with a note from me saying, "Helen is obviously irritated by your slow response on this issue. Could you please tell her when you will be making a decision?" Then I'd copy the forwarded e-mail and note back to the sender. I'm sure more than one colleague must have choked on their coffee.

What my impatient colleagues didn't know was that I immediately pulled the e-mail from Jack Welch's box before he saw it. Sue would urge me to call the offenders to let them know that they could climb back in off the ledge outside their office window and return to work. "I'll call in a couple of hours," I'd say, making sure the lesson stuck.

Of course, I could have fired off a memo confronting the executive directly, but it might have caused hard feelings. A bit of humor, showing the offending executive the error of his or her ways, was more effective.

PHONE GAMES

My e-mail sting worked every time because it played to the latent fear that the people who work with top management will abuse their positions. Capriciousness and overprotectiveness can be a real headache and frustration. I'd guess that the day after Alexander Graham Bell invented the telephone, assistants started playing the old game of Put Him on First, or PHOF. The object is to force the receiving caller's assistant to put his or her boss on the line before the incoming party is connected. There's status to be won if you get to hand off a call to your boss without having him sullied by exposure to the other guy's assistant. As in chess, the opening move is crucial. A senior PHOF player simply refuses to connect a call unless the other party is on the line. Period. There's nothing to be done about it short of hanging up and telling your boss that the person he wanted to talk to is dead. I tended not to fight this if the caller or the callee was an esteemed business leader of great seniority and prestige, like Warren Buffett. (Mr. Buffett, by the way, was more than likely to have dialed his own call.) On the other hand, if the éminence grise wanted Jack Welch on the line first, so be it. For others, if I was feeling ornery, I might point out that "Mr. Welch is returning the call," implying that only a bad-mannered, self-important gatekeeper would insist on PHOF when her boss is the one who called us in the first place! But I'm not a serious player. Most of the time, I put the other person on hold and say, "I've got his assistant on the line and she's being a phone meanie. She insists that you have to be on the line before he comes on."

The reaction was predictable—he'd roll his eyes, followed by a chuckle from both of us as he picked up the phone and said, "Hi, this is Jack Welch," without a trace of exasperation or irascibility.

When I was on the phone with extremely powerful corporate executives, I was always on my best behavior, which included conducting a little diplomatic outreach whenever appropriate. By keeping up with the top business publications and broadcasts, I was aware of positive coverage and prominently displayed interviews with industry leaders. If we had to wait until Jack finished another call to pick up, I'd say something like "That was a wonderful profile of your company in *Business Week*, Mr. Bennett," or I'd simultaneously call up his company's stock on my computer and say, "You must be pleased that your stock is at a fifty-two-week high." (The lows were studiously ignored.) Nothing of real substance, but I was killing time and letting the caller know that he was on our radarscope and that we followed the fortunes of his company. In instances when a senior executive had dialed his own call and Jack wasn't available, I'd share a little inside information: "Mr. Welch will be sorry he missed your call, but he is in the conference room with a rather large crowd doing a strategy review. Can I have him call you back this afternoon?" By explaining why the call wasn't being taken, the caller might feel a little better than if I had just coldly refused. It also is a down payment on getting the caller to be forthcoming about the reason he or she wanted to talk to Jack. I tried to obtain at least the general context for the call so that I could pull out any needed background research and have it available for him when he returned the call.

A cold and aloof phone style has its place, I suppose, but I found that a little warmth and a human touch produces good results and tangible benefits in productivity. Staying on top of business developments can add to your effectiveness when it comes to managing up, as does staying closely attuned to the who, what, when, where, and why of your own operation. Sounding out of it usually means only one thing—you *are* out of it.

HITTING THE WALL

About once a month—and often coinciding with a full moon— strange calls and callers would work their way through the GE filtering system and find their way to my desk. Due to Jack's high public profile, we were contacted by people who are drawn to celebrities and political figures. They had schemes to save the world, ideas about broadcasting Bible history in prime time on NBC, and surefire inventions that just needed a few million dollars in seed money. A toy inventor called practically every night for a month demanding to talk to Jack Welch about backing his latest toy concept. He must have read somewhere that if you call after six or seven o'clock there's a chance that a senior executive who is working late might pick up his own phone. But not in our operation. That happened to Jack once, early in his tenure as CEO. He got stuck with an irate washing-machine owner, and learned his lesson. Caller ID came in very handy in being a little more cautious about picking up unidentified non-GE calls after hours. I listened to the toy inventor and promised to pass his information along, but he took to berating me as "Miss BAD-owski" and threatening to tell Jack how mean and awful I was.

I did have a soft spot for the angry appliance customers. It made me feel like I was making a connection to the old GE to hear how someone's dishwasher wasn't going into the rinse cycle, and what was Jack Welch going to do about it? I referred them to a special number that our appliance business in Louisville had set up to respond to calls like theirs. A keen and very responsive operation, they answered with this line: "The chairman's office . . ." The ones who just wanted to vent, I would listen to them go on, and think, *Madam, not in your worst nightmare would you want Jack Welch to drive up to your front door with a screwdriver in hand to fix your precious washing machine. Then you would* really *have something to complain about.*

GEMS

GE is still so identified with light bulbs and consumer appliances that many people are surprised to learn that GE is one of the largest makers of industrial diamonds. An offshoot of this business is a specialty line of natural gem-quality, jewelry-grade diamonds. Our researchers developed a method of finishing the natural conversion process of brown diamonds to clear and gleaming gems fit for any type of jewelry setting. In his memoir, *Jack: Straight from the Gut,* Jack Welch related how the company got into this business in 1998, despite the fierce opposition of the old-line Antwerp traders and wholesalers, who had controlled the diamond market for centuries.

Jack really caught diamond fever. He gave the start-up venture a lot of time and attention. Instead of the usual briefcases bulging with documents, our diamond executives would troop into his office for meetings carrying simple plastic boxes containing thousands of dollars' worth of gorgeous diamonds of various sizes and cuts. One afternoon shortly after a meeting broke up, I heard, "Oh, shit—Ro, come here."[1]

I shot into the conference room to find Jack on his knees on the floor frantically hunting for six or seven diamonds that he had knocked off the table. A jewel box was overturned and empty; the gems had scattered and hidden themselves in the pile of the carpeting, under the table, and beneath a couple of the conference chairs.

"What happened?" I asked.

"My hand slipped, the box flipped, and . . . ," he trailed off sheepishly.

The two of us played find-the-diamonds for quite a while, crawling around on all fours, laughing, until we recovered all the gems. The bigger ones were not a problem, but the smaller gems were very hard to find. Fortunately, every diamond was logged on an inventory sheet, so we knew exactly what was missing. I had visions of the cleaning staff sucking up the equivalent of my annual salary with a couple of passes of the vacuum cleaner. I wasn't going to leave the room until the search-and-rescue was completed.

To date, the diamond business has been slower to catch fire for GE than expected. Company employees get to buy them at a discount, though. I treated myself to a pair of diamond earrings as a reward for twenty-five years of having to wear panty hose every day. Of course, diamond studs are just the thing to accent the telephone receiver that is permanently stuck to my ear, and for getting dolled up for my formal evenings of trekking to the all-night car wash. But it's true that diamonds do go with everything. Even with the basic dark suits that dominate my wardrobe.

I did occasionally accent my workaday wardrobe with a grand display of rhinestones. For years I kept a cheap, glittery rhinestone tiara in my desk drawer to bring out when we needed a mood brightener. In my tiara, I was the queen bee. I usually did it to crack up Sue or an occasional office visitor, though sometimes I did a royal walkabout on the third floor, passing by in state splendor and giving the haughty royal wave. It had to be a very slow day for such antics, and one where I'd encounter no important visitors. But my queen bee act was a way to deliberately puncture the isolation and, yes, the pomposity that can be associated with life at the high rung of the corporate ladder. The queen bee's message was *Don't forget who I really am; we're all on the same team.* I took my job seriously, but I didn't take myself seriously. Consequently, the wall around the CEO's office was a lot lower and less forbidding than it otherwise might have been. Informality was very important to Jack. He saw it as an important management tool. Informality breaks down barriers and enhances communication. Laughter and informality go hand in hand.

But even when I put away my rhinestone tiara, I still wielded a scepter. I was keeper of the remote control device that opened and closed the large sliding door to Jack Welch's office. He had a remote too, but most of the time when there was a private meeting under way, I would slide the door shut at the beginning and open it as the session began to break up. At other times, the door tended to stay open. The exceptions were the moments when Jack was more vociferous than usual. I'd put up with it as long as I could and then hit the close button. The doors would silently glide shut and there'd be a moment's peace. He'd get me back, though, by waiting for moments when I was telling him something he'd rather not hear. In midsentence, the door would close. I'd hit the remote and open it again, but he'd hit close. We'd go back and forth dueling with the door. At that point, I'd leave it closed . . . a quiet break for me.

PICTURE THIS

Occasionally, my sense of humor is misunderstood. Jack was being featured in an issue of *Modern Maturity*, the magazine published by the American Association of Retired Persons. They sent a photographer to our office to get pictures to go with the article. Having been on hand for dozens of photo shoots, I know how stiff and glum people start looking as they stand around waiting for the photographer to compose his artistic shots. Most photographers banter a little with their subjects to loosen them up, but the guy from *Modern Maturity* was Mr. Serious. Rather than have Jack staring blankly into the camera or trying to keep an artificial smile locked on his face, I started making a few jokes to lighten the mood. When the photographer suggested he stand behind a chair, I said, "For this magazine, pretend it's a walker and hold on to the back." That broke everybody up except the photographer, who yelled at me, "Will you be quiet!" And that worked like a charm. Instantly everybody went from smiles back to frowns and stiffness. I do try to get the last word, though. "Oh I'm sorry, I didn't realize you were using an *audio* camera." He just glowered at me.

There must be thousands of individual photographs of Jack Welch, but as far as I know, there's only one bronze bust. In 1993 he was chosen by *CEO Magazine* to be CEO of the year, an honor that is accompanied by having a bronze bust (technically it was not a bust, just the head) commissioned for the magazine's private collection. Jack was leery of the idea but finally agreed. The bronze arrived in time for a big meeting in Fairfield of GE executives. Sue and I set up a table right outside the meeting room near the door. We draped the table with a linen cloth and set the head in the middle surrounded by flowers. Everybody who came to the meeting had to pass by the "shrine." It was a mild tease, but served to let the gang appreciate the honor in a lighthearted way, without Jack being embarrassed by the fuss and pretentiousness of a formal unveiling. At least we didn't use it as a doorstop.

WHITE KNUCKLES

We were flying back from Colorado in 1992 after Jack gave a speech to a management team at a General Mills conference. Upon take-off, one of our plane's wheels flew off the aircraft due to a flaw in the metal of the landing gear. The pilots decided to fly back toward New York and deal with equipment failure a little closer to home rather than try to set the plane down in Colorado. We had intended to do office work on the plane the entire flight home. Knowing there was nothing we could do for several hours, Jack decided to continue with the work we had planned to do on the return flight.

I was trying to concentrate on the work but was more concerned with our damaged aircraft. I said to him, only half in jest, "If we're going to crash-land when we get to New York, why am I spending the last three hours of my life *working*?" Jack gave me a prolonged, pensive look, closed up the files and papers at the work-table, and put them away. We moved up front, reviewed the crash landing and physical escape procedures with the flight attendant, and fretted all the way home. For the last half hour before landing, Jack jumped between his seat and the cockpit, reviewing the status of the reports from the control tower as the flight crew tried to assess the damage to the landing gear. We were met on the runway at Stuart Air Force Base in upstate New York with fire trucks and firefighters with silver suits ready to foam down the plane upon landing if necessary. Although we were all nervous, we joked non-stop on our approach to calm our nerves. Straightening up in our seats from the crash position after a safe landing, I was glad to know, looking back, that we dealt with that situation with humor instead of hysteria.

Managing up can probably be accomplished without humor. But why would you want to? And I'm not so sure that you can manage up to anywhere near maximum effect without it. Grimness and gloom can be immense burdens. There's nothing that lightens the load like a little laughter.

To demonstrate how serious I am about humor, I'll close with yet another maxim: If at the end of the day you haven't laughed, you've wasted the day. And that's bad business indeed.[2]

Humor Takeaways

- Lack of laughter is a sign of a business *in* trouble, headed *for* trouble, or that deserves *to be* in trouble.
- Laugh and the world will laugh with you—and if they don't, you're still better off.
- Don't let other people's power or position intimidate you—use humor to respectfully level the playing field.
- Don't take yourself too seriously.

CHAPTER 8

Common Sense

I HAD ONLY BEEN working with Jack Welch for a couple of months when I encountered a piece of common sense that still serves as my operational Rock of Gibraltar.

I was in the middle of a reasonably important assignment, though I can't remember precisely what—something that was dropped in my lap, no doubt, along with a dozen other tasks. But before I could finish, Jack called me into his office to give me yet another task. I stood there in front of the wall of windows that looked out on a green and leafy Connecticut hillside, and without first stopping to think, I told him I would do it as soon as I got through with his previous request. In other words, *Please take a number and get in line.*

Mistake. In his typically straightforward way, Jack simply pointed out that if things were going to work out in the future, my job was to do what he wanted when he wanted it done—not what I wanted when I wanted it done. Finishing one task before starting another was what I wanted, and would have made my life easier. However, what he wanted was to move on to the next issue right then and there. My role, as he saw it, was to drop what I was doing and make what he wanted happen. He was the pace car—it was my job to keep up.

Now, step back a moment to examine this comment, which on the surface at least seems to be symptomatic of terminal egomania. Actually, though, I think Jack revealed to me a key component of a major business philosophy: The boss comes first.

And it is pure, invaluable common sense. Whether they admit it or not, most businesses are hierarchical organizations, more feudal in structure than democratic. By recognizing this and seeing to it that the person we report to comes first, just as the person one rung below endeavors to do the same for us, a chain of service, leadership, and responsibility is forged. The benefits flow up and down the chain. Sure, the chain can be broken. There are bad managers and bad employees. But this semifeudal model has a lot going for it. For one thing, it works.

I can't recall reading news reports about companies that top the "best places to work" lists in magazines one day and face bankruptcy proceedings the next. The good companies tend to last. When the boss comes first, it doesn't stifle individualism and excellence; rather, it allows all the other stars to shine more brightly. We win when the boss wins; the boss wins when we win.

When those above you win, you win.

For many people, it's difficult—very difficult—to overcome an ingrained resentment toward authority. By and large, that's probably a good thing. It makes us strong and independent. But it can also lead to alienation and uncooperativeness, which is one reason so much time and thought have gone into management theories for working around people problems. Reinventing the workplace, casual Fridays, innovative training programs, Silicon Valley–style informality, flattening the organization, mentoring, and teamwork, to name just a few, are attempts to find new and better techniques to motivate workers to excel at what they do on the job.

Fine. Get a mentor, join a team, and focus hard on your career development; there's nothing wrong with any of that. But I believe one of the quickest ways to excel is also one of the oldest ways: Go to work for someone who excels and help that person achieve even more excellence.

Did it hurt my self-esteem to know that during the course of a workday what Jack Welch wanted took precedence over what I wanted? No. I could see the results all around me as the company grew and prospered. And you know what? Maybe I had a small role in its success. If nothing else, it made me feel good to be part of a winning team, and I was well rewarded for my work. If the team had been a bunch of losers and the boss a jerk, I would have had a classic remedy at my disposal: I could have (and would have) gone to work someplace else.

Forgive me if I sound like my mother (or your mother). This is very old-fashioned doctrine that I'm spouting. The reason that I was able to form such an effective working partnership with Jack Welch may be explained by his roots in working-class Salem, Massachusetts, and mine in blue-collar Bridgeport, Connecticut. Despite our age difference, we essentially came from the same social stratum with many values and attitudes in common. My mother and his were similar in important ways. They were strong-willed, independent, forthright women. Like Grace Welch, Tekla Badowski was the CEO in our household, and the woman you went to in the neighborhood to get things done. She was the neighborhood seamstress, barber, baby-tooth puller, tax advisor, chef, baker, party planner, and entertainer. Mom had a genius for improvisation. One summer, six relatives from Canada whom she hadn't seen for thirty years called from the local Howard Johnson's to say hi and ask if they could stay for the weekend at our house. Within an hour, she had rounded up as many local relatives as she could find, arranged for an instant family reunion, and provided lodging for the Canadian contingent—all on zero notice. Nothing rattled her; nothing was insurmountable. She evaluated what needed to be done, drew up a plan, and implemented it, step by step.

My father, Johnny, was a metal polisher at Casco Corporation. At home, he was quieter than Mom, steady, and totally no-nonsense, much the way John Welch Sr. had been. Not much riled Dad. He was easygoing and nonpolitical. He was on call weekends and evenings as the neighborhood plumber, carpenter, electrician, bricklayer, and landscaper. Today he'd be a Home Depot guru's guru. He could build, fix, or solve *almost* anything. I have to qualify the statement due to a slight mishap removing a huge bees' nest in a bush in front of my aunt and uncle's house. Dad used a chemical hornet and wasp spray, but he didn't take the warning label about flammability seriously. To finish the job right, he set fire to the nest. Instantly, we had a real-life burning bush appear, and it almost took Aunt Ceil and Uncle Ray's house with it. The Bridgeport fire department got a chance to display their shiny equipment that day. Dad got teased about it for years, but he took it with good humor.

My parents were basic, uncomplicated people who went to work each day, balanced family responsibilities without a lot of fuss, and had no time for theorizing about life or second-guessing themselves. They lived the Nike slogan, "Just do it," before Nike thought of it.

I think that's the reason Jack Welch's commonsense approach to business struck such a responsive chord in me. I wasn't a stranger to his world, nor was he to mine. In our worlds, it's better to support the boss than to thwart the boss. Doing your best is second nature. Winning is important; agonizing and soul-searching are not. Don't make the same mistake twice. What's done is done. Eat on the run and go to the bathroom when you have a chance, because you might not have time later. And don't take yourself too seriously.

Winning is important.

COMMON SENSE FROM MAE

Another primary source of common sense in my life came from Mae Sancibrian. Mae was my business teacher at Notre Dame Catholic High School and an early mentor. A woman of many facets, she was strong and disciplined, demanded your best performance, and yet had a soft, encouraging, fun, and passionate side. Mae pushed us hard and didn't settle for less than our best work.

She had experience in the real world of business, and so she taught her students things we didn't get from the textbooks. Mae used to say, "You can go on a job interview typing a hundred words a minute and taking shorthand at two hundred, but if you walk in there wearing Murray Space Shoes [Murray Space was a local manufacturer of ugly orthopedic footwear], you'll never get the job." What she was telling us was that hiring decisions are based on many different factors—personality, skill, appearance. You could have the best technical skills around, but the complementary things help you get and keep a job.

My colleague Sue Baye was also one of her students. We'd laugh and compare notes on Mrs. Sancibrian, who after many years in the classroom returned to the world of business. She worked at GE for a while and eventually in the office of the CEO of Xerox. She'd call us every couple of years to see how we were doing, proud that two of her former students had made it to the top at GE.

I might be working at the U.S. Customs Service if it wasn't for Mae. She waged a one-woman campaign to convince my parents and me that I should accept a two-year scholarship at Sacred Heart University. I had been offered a job at Customs right out of high school. Mrs. Sancibrian told my parents that the surprise scholarship was an opportunity I couldn't pass up. I took the scholarship, went for two years and got an associate's degree, and by then had enough common sense of my own to continue on nights and weekends to get a bachelor's degree.

WHAT HAVE YOU DONE FOR ME LATELY?

In May 1996, I hit a milestone at GE. It was my twentieth anniversary of walking into the legal department law library for my first day on the job. Sue Baye also celebrated her twentieth year at GE that May, so to cause trouble and annoy Jack Welch, I asked him if he would make a special presentation of our gifts to mark the occasion. And I got the answer I expected: a gruff, end-of-subject no.

"Then can you take us out to lunch?"

"No."

"Can I at least take Sue out to lunch?"

"No." This may have been one of those times that he pushed the remote control button to close the sliding office door.

When our service day arrived, I said, "Happy twentieth, Sue."

"Happy twentieth, Rosanne."

And we went back to work. Neither of us really expected lunch or a special presentation. I was just pulling Jack's chain. He had a long-standing thing against making a big fuss over longevity. He believed that it made more sense to recognize employees for what they were doing this year, this month, this week than for the fact that they had been around for fifteen or twenty or forty-five years. It was another example of his emphasis on the present rather than the past.

It may seem to be an odd attitude for a guy who spent more than forty years working for GE, but I see it as totally consistent with his philosophy and his streak of common sense. As a young executive, he had been exposed to his share of corporate veterans whose glory days were long over but who continued to hold on to power. A "what have you done for me lately?" policy may seem cruel, but is it kind to encumber a corporation and its talented, hard-charging workforce with deadwood? That sort of kindness kills businesses and jobs.

The "Neutron Jack" label that was applied by the press in the mid-1980s rankled him—and still does—because he was being unfairly criticized for having the courage and common sense to do the right thing. Neutron bombs were designed to eliminate people and leave buildings and infrastructure intact. It made for a dramatic—and misguided—analogy by the press for the downsizing and layoffs that were under way at the time at GE under Jack's leadership. As painful as the job losses were, it wasn't Armageddon. If anything, I saw it as drastically needed surgery that saved the company from a disease that could have cost far more jobs and caused severe long-term repercussions. Easy for me to say, of course. I had a job. But I can imagine my father saying what I'm about to add: If I'd lost that job, I'd have found another one. It may take longer in today's market to find the right situation, but jobs are out there.

CEOs are paid to look after the health of their companies. Without growth, increasing profits, new products and services, and bright prospects for expanding market share, a company will get sick and die. By refusing to change direction and make adjustments, the jobs that are temporarily saved are doomed in the long run. And they doom those that might have survived in a leaner, more aggressive and nimble operation. It was all entirely consistent with Jack Welch's commonsense emphasis on nurturing people. Is it better to have an anemic, struggling company with a flabby payroll of the dispirited, unmotivated, and the disappointed, or one that's a third or half its size full of supercharged, creative, and satisfied people?

The answer came about ten years later as "Neutron Jack" gave way to "Icon Jack" to coincide with the emergence of GE as the world's largest and most profitable corporation at that time. Although the dot-com meltdown and recession that followed crimped our stock price, as a company, GE withstood the economic storm in good shape.

The boom of the mid-1990s ended with such a sudden bust, it would be an exaggeration to say that Jack Welch saw it coming—but not much of an exaggeration. In the winter of 2000–2001, he told one key Washington policymaker that, based on what he was seeing internally at GE, trouble was brewing in the economy at large. Our customers were cutting back on orders and drawing down their inventories. The numbers were off. GE is such a large company, covering so many different sectors, that its activity or lack of it can be a reasonably reliable indicator for the rest of the economy. As CEO, he was sitting on a mountain of fresh, real-time data that government and private economists would have loved to get their hands on to crunch, slice, and dice for their projections.

Despite the dark clouds, there was no sense of panic, even when the stock dropped sharply from previous highs. I know Jack felt badly for shareholders and those GE employees with stock options and their savings in stock plans, but his attitude was that there had been many ups and downs in the past, and there was no reason to see it as anything more than part of a cycle that, in due course, would head higher. Given that I was familiar with his personal stock portfolio and extensive GE holdings, I was amazed that on bad days in the market, when he might have suffered personal losses of—I'm guessing—tens of millions of dollars, he didn't show any sign of irritability. He had such confidence in the strength of the company that he'd just ignore the losses and go about his business.

However, in the middle of the bull market we all got pretty giddy as GE share prices climbed higher and higher. If it was necessary to interrupt a meeting, I had a habit of handing him whatever message required his immediate attention, along with a separate note about the latest stock price. He usually shared the price with the group; if it had gone to a new high, there would be a cheer and applause.

The day the price broke 100, I made several forays into a meeting room with a series of updates as the value inched upward. As it approached the magic number, there was a chant from the group of "Go, Ro, go." I printed up some large sheets of paper displaying the numbers and held them through the crack in the door like an Olympic figure-skating judge.

Although my personal stock portfolio is relatively small, its backbone is made up of GE stock and, of course, stock options I was fortunate to have been awarded. Options came in for a lot of criticism after the dot-com collapse. It was under Jack Welch's leadership at GE that options were made available, on a merit basis, to a much broader cross-section of the company's workforce. Until he came along, options were reserved for top management. He felt that performance should be rewarded and a portion of the wealth shared by those who helped create it. I understand that one prominent senior executive who retired long ago was very put out when the decision was made to offer options to the staff. Whenever the subject of options comes up, Jack Welch points with pride to all the orthodontist bills, college tuitions, home mortgages, and retirement nest eggs they helped underwrite. An option is a way to share in a company's success. To me, that's nothing more than simple, old-fashioned common sense.

In my early years on the job, I assumed that Jack was a great (non-GE) stock picker based on his incredible business savvy—common sense, right? It's uncanny how adept he was at spotting trends weeks before the business publications started to write about them. I was surprised at how little he played the stock market, but since I placed buy and sell orders for him with his broker, I would tag along to purchase a few shares of my own of whatever he was buying. This didn't happen very often, I should add, because the GE legal department has stringent reporting requirements in order to stay on the lawful side of Securities and Exchange Commission trading regulations. Usually, it was just too troublesome to frequently buy or sell stock, as far as I was concerned. But as for Jack Welch, stock picker extraordinaire—forget it. I would have done better buying lottery tickets.

MANAGING UP WITH COMMON SENSE

Common sense is difficult to write about convincingly because it can sound so commonplace and boring, or be way too subtle. Here are five nuggets of common sense that fall somewhere in between:

1. *It's over when it's over.* A slogan attributed to Yogi Berra that became popular in the 1990s, "It ain't over till it's over," is a useful motivator, but be careful not to take it too far. Better to move ahead than dwell on bad decisions and mistakes.

2. *Don't make people decisions lightly.* They are the most important decisions you will make. Organizations do not run on money, products, or processes. (It's the people, stupid.)

3. *Trust your instincts.* Overanalysis can lead to paralysis.

4.   *Don't* always *trust your instincts.* Instincts are formed by experience. If you're new on the job, check your gut feelings at the door until you have accumulated enough experience to let your instincts come into play.
5.   *Go ahead, take a swing.* It's better to be faulted for being too bold than too timid. Jack Welch taught me that.

Finally, one from the Delphic oracle: Know thyself. Do you know your strengths and weaknesses? If not, I'd suggest you start thinking about them. It's only common sense. And you can't manage up effectively without it.

WILL HE OR WON'T HE?

In the spring of 1994, a full seven years before he would turn sixty-five years old, Jack Welch initiated a process for finding a successor as CEO and chairman of GE. He could have waited until retirement was a couple of years away, handpicked an heir, or simply dusted off the succession process that his predecessor had used. But Jack had too much common sense for that.

In his memoir, Jack Welch was extremely careful in the way he presented the "horse race" that he had participated in and ultimately won in 1981 to get the top job at GE. But I don't have to be quite as careful. I know he hated that horse race, the anguish it inflicted on those who were running in it, and the disruption it caused to the smooth working of GE's top management. My guess is that he intended as far back as 1981 to design a high-quality succession process typical of GE, and one that has since served as a model for other large corporations.

But what do I know? And I'm not being coy. I haven't discussed it with him. My view is based on watching the process up close as it unfolded. I'll focus on it in a little more depth in Chapter 14, when I deal with teamwork. Right now, though, I want to point out that the long lead time he provided allowed for a smooth, thorough process to take place without the "Will he or won't he leave?" uncertainty that could have been destabilizing. From 1994 on, the message was clear: A new team, a new generation would take the company into the twenty-first century.

However, I have to admit that I was a little skeptical. In 1997 during a particularly hectic period, burnout got the better of me one afternoon. I said to him, "If there's a chance you'll change your mind and work until you're seventy, I'd like to know now so that I can quit but still give you enough time to train a replacement to take you through the next ten years." On the other hand, if I knew for sure that he would retire at sixty-five and not a day later, I said I'd commit to sticking it out until then.

Jack assured me he was determined to retire at sixty-five. I said, "If that's true, I want it in writing." I grabbed a paper and pen and put them in front of him. He wrote out: "To Rosanne—I will not work past 11/19/2000 for GE." My demand must have gotten his attention, because he actually spelled my name correctly, something he has trouble with to this day.

I stayed on. And I should have had enough common sense to know that the document would turn out to be worthless.

Common Sense Takeaways

- Your boss's agenda comes first. Period.
- When those above you win, you win.
- It's people! Organizations don't run on money, products, or procedures.
- Trust your instincts—they are based on a lot of experience. Then again, don't *always* trust your instincts.
- Go ahead, take a swing: Better to be too bold than too timid.

CHAPTER 9

Preparedness

ANYONE WHO ASPIRES to be effective at managing up should send a hefty donation to the Boy Scouts to cover the cost of renting their motto. "Be prepared" says it all.

Half of my life while working side by side with Jack Welch was spent preparing for the other half of my life. Preparation made up the bulk of my business activity, and like the submerged part of an iceberg, it was hidden beneath the surface of everyday events.

Success is 80 percent preparation.

Often, what to fellow CEOs or GE's major customers appeared to be a casual, unplanned encounter with Jack Welch was underpinned by hours of phone calls and a long string of e-mails that they would never know about. Roughly two weeks prior to a Business Council meeting, for instance, I would start preparing. Based in Washington, D.C., the Business Council is a prestigious, invitation-only group of top corporate leaders that meets three times a year in varying locations to exchange views among themselves and with government representatives. In other words, they dine, drink, and talk serious business.

It was reasonably easy to predict whom Jack would be rubbing shoulders with when he attended: a whole lot of important customers and potential customers, suppliers and other partners, and a mixed bag of close friends, closely watched competitors, and assorted government officials. I'd alert our business units to the upcoming meeting with a memo requesting that they send a summary overview of pending deals and activities with companies whose leaders were also members of the Business Council.

Simple, right? No, it wasn't as easy as it sounds. Even though I emphasized in my request that we needed only one or two pages, some of our units responded by turning in briefing books the size of the Manhattan telephone directory.

In a way, I couldn't blame them for the data overload. Here was an opportunity to get the message across and leave no stone unturned, no detail left to the imagination. What we were hoping for was to have ammo (that's why they're called bullets, right?) that Jack could use in his one-on-one encounters with the other business leaders. Most of the time that would happen at cocktail parties, dinner, or on the fly in a hotel lobby or hallway.

I guess what our people didn't understand was that Jack Welch was not going to be able to present those detailed bar graphs, pie charts, and spreadsheets, filled to the bursting point with five years' worth of statistics, while he balanced a glass of red wine in one hand and a plate of hors d'oeuvres in the other.

What he used this material for was to raise key points to jar loose an issue that might have been stalled or perhaps was causing a delay in some negotiations. Or he would offer a couple of suggestions for breaking an impasse or solving a problem. The bullet points that were collected gave Jack a feel for the current state of a given situation. Frequently, just an expression of interest on his part was well received by another CEO.

Occasionally, I played the role of editor and took my yellow highlighter to submitted material that was in need of pruning. I'd try to choose the key points based on my familiarity with what Jack Welch generally regarded as significant data. I would base my judgment on listening to the kinds of questions he often asked of senior executives. He was always interested in outcomes: "Where is this headed? Where do we expect to end up? What do we project?" And I taught myself to read business documents, not as Rosanne Badowski would, but as though I were Jack Welch. By observing what he gleaned from the original beyond what I had excerpted, I was able to get a feel for how deep he would go to dig out data and what types of corroborating material he would rely on. This helped me consolidate briefing material for him in the future.

PREFLIGHT

You don't have to be a fortune-teller to be good at prepping your boss. Try looking at his or her calendar. Each item calls for a little or a lot of preparation. If you're not doing it, who is? If you are a vice chairman, the chairman may be able to use your input for tomorrow's meeting. The same thing applies whatever your title and wherever you fit into the hierarchy. Share what you have, share what you know. Don't wait for an invitation. Too many hands never spoiled preparation soup.

Preparing Jack Welch was one of my major daily tasks. There was rarely an event on his calendar that didn't require some kind of groundwork other than logistical arrangements. I had to ask and answer questions like these:

- What's the purpose of the meeting or event?
- Who is involved?
- What contribution is JW expected to make?
- What's on the agenda?
- What information does JW need to have regarding the players and the issues?
- Does JW need input from others prior to the event? If so, who and what?
- Is the focus of this event likely to extend to other matters? If so, what are they?
- What kind of follow-up is likely?
- Who needs to be informed?
- Are there other non-agenda areas and subjects that JW could profitably pursue?

Everyone should have their own mental preflight checklist shaped to a large degree by the boss's personality and the dynamics of his or her business. Some people might not feel comfortable trying to digest the amount of data that Jack could handle. On the other hand, they may not possess the ability to improvise as skillfully as he did (thanks in large part to an excellent memory). It was comforting for me to know that if I inadvertently left some gaps uncovered, he'd be able to wing it or say, "I don't know. I'll get back to you in the morning on that." For an executive with a brain that soaked up information like a sponge, he never had any qualms about admitting that he didn't have an answer at his fingertips.

ANNUAL MEETINGS

Fortunately, I was spared the mother of all prep jobs. By the time I came along in the job, Jack Welch no longer obsessed about getting ready for the annual shareholders' meetings. Early in his tenure as CEO, he spent weeks perfecting his keynote address and bracing himself to handle the chores of the ringmaster in a thirty-three-ring circus, including taking questions from the floor from shareholders and moderating the obligatory airing of friendly and unfriendly, informed and uninformed, intelligent and silly viewpoints.

My first annual meeting while I was Jack's executive assistant was his eighth as CEO (I didn't attend but observed the prep). By then he had stopped assuming that it was necessary to know everything about every subject that might come up. Plus, in 1989, the tide of critical press coverage had begun to shift away from downsizing (which was over for the most part) and toward emphasizing the major acquisitions GE was making. Even so, he probably worked on and off for two weeks preparing for the annual meeting, which was held in Greenville, South Carolina. The site was chosen because it was a GE town—our gas turbine business is headquartered there. Usually, GE held the annual meeting in cities where we had GE facilities, such as Milwaukee, Louisville, and Fort Wayne, but that were off the beaten track. Yet there was always a contingent of the irate-about-something on hand.

Jack Welch isn't a flamboyant formal orator and doesn't pretend to be one. His favorite speaking mode is a short introduction followed by questions and answers. However, the annual meetings demanded a prepared speech. Most of the content was drawn from his "Letter from the Chairman," included in each GE annual report.

Jack wrote most of that himself with the help of speechwriter Bill Lane, who took the ideas they discussed and put them into a first draft. The revision process took a month or more, with as many as thirty different versions emerging. Each letter conveyed an important message, which was eagerly awaited and analyzed by businesspeople and investors from around the world. Jack was passionate about getting it right. I assisted by trying to look at the document from the perspective of the average stockholder. If the wording wasn't clear and easily understandable, I flagged it and would explain why it didn't make sense to me. Critiquing Jack's writing style may seem presumptuous, but he encouraged me to speak up. Unlike his bold, never-look-back decision-making style, he labored hard over the written words to get them just right. We'd often try out subtly different sentence structures to see which one worked best, the way a shopper would try on several pairs of new shoes to find the best fit.

This is an area where those who are managing up can be of real service. As long as the person at the next level has the confidence to accept suggestions, judicious editing of his or her written material to help make the presentation simple and clear is a triple win. The boss wins by gaining a reputation as an effective communicator; the reader wins by getting a powerful message, and you win because the boss wins.

The timing of the writing of the annual report letter was such that it coincided with our yearly European business reviews, which took place the last week in January. I spent many hours in Europe not sightseeing but revising the letter again and again in a car, office, or hotel room (in addition to the regular workload). When we got back home, the printing deadline fortunately ruled out a lot more tinkering. After that, it was relatively easy to rework the letter into a speech format for the annual meeting.

As a measure of its importance, Jack Welch actually rehearsed the speech, mainly to clock the time it took to read it. Although he never used a Teleprompter at the meetings, his delivery was smooth and forceful, as if he knew and believed every word of it. And you know what? He did. Delivering those messages was very important to him.

Personally, I had mixed feelings about the annual shareholders' meetings. Major investors didn't bother attending, and I felt bad for the enthusiastic legitimate small shareholders who came ready to immerse themselves in the GE culture but had to put up with vocal special-interest groups and single-issue crusaders. Every year there was an open forum to allow shareholders to ask questions of the CEO—in theory a fine idea. But in practice, many of the questions turned into rambling diatribes on subjects irrelevant to GE. Jack had to chair these talkathons. I could tell he would have loved to debate some of the issues, particularly when it came to the inaccurate charges that GE was harming the environment. However, he successfully fought the urge and would ignore the speaker's attempts to engage him. "Thank you," he'd say blandly. "Will the next speaker come to the microphone, please?" By not rising to the bait but still allowing the speakers to sound off, he allowed contrary views to be heard without paralyzing an orderly process.

Furthermore, from a public relations standpoint, it was a sound strategy. Slugging it out with the protesters would have distracted the press's attention from the keynote speech that laid out his vision for the upcoming year and put the preceding twelve months in perspective.

THE PRESS GANG

On balance, Jack Welch got great press coverage. Was this the result of preparation, luck, or bribery? Naturally, I think it was preparation. But the real answer is none of the above. The ratio of all the positive or neutral press clippings compared to the actual time spent preparing to deal with the news media was extremely lop-sided, to the point that you could easily conclude that the favorable coverage just happened on its own accord and that the preparation had nothing to do with it. Of course, that's absurd in this day and age of spin and media hypermanagement. GE has an effective public relations department that was both proactive and reactive on Jack's behalf. Yet he spent relatively little time worrying about how the news media would portray him. Jack had cordial relations with the press, particularly in the 1990s, but managing the press was not one of his management hats.

One of the dividends of being well prepared in terms of what was going on at GE was that it gave him the facts, figures, and real-life examples he needed when he was contacted by reporters. That eliminated the need for the kind of boning-up sessions that some CEOs go through to prepare for interviews and news conferences. In recent years, a breed of media consultant has sprung up that specializes in training business executives to deal with the press. Hours are spent anticipating questions and rehearsing answers into video cameras to perfect facial expressions, gestures, and eye contact.

Jack Welch didn't do that. What he did do, though, was read the newspapers religiously and watch TV in the evenings and on week-ends (we had a TV set in the office but didn't turn it on unless there was breaking news). The car that picked him up at home each morning had *The New York Times, The Wall Street Journal,* and other major papers. (The tabloid *New York Post* found its way into the pile, too, in order to satisfy Jack's thirst for juicy gossip.) On the ride to the office, he looked first at the articles that dealt with GE and some-times immediately picked up the phone to call the head of GE Public Relations to find out what was being done (if the story was negative or incomplete) and to discuss options for press follow-up.

Inaccurate or unfair stories were more than just hard on the ego. They could hurt employee morale and affect the price of GE stock.

These two factors prompted Jack to pay close attention to what the news media were writing and saying. Wall Street analysts and the rest of the investment community rely so heavily on the press for information that it's extremely important to correct the record quickly and to provide the company's perspective in a timely fashion. Most of the time, it doesn't do any good to complain about inaccuracies or squabble with the press. But on one occasion, a reporter assigned to cover GE for a major newspaper got himself in trouble. His stories seemed to be more a reflection of his personal point of view than a straightforward account of what was really going on. Fed up, Jack decided he would no longer grant him interviews. When GE is your primary beat, that's a major problem, and when the journalist realized what was happening, he pleaded for access—to no avail. Jack was adamant, knowing that before long the reporter's editors would start wondering why their guy wasn't getting access to GE's high-profile chairman. He was finally reassigned, and his replacement had no trouble obtaining interviews and comments from then on.

I tried to keep my distance from the press by referring media calls and e-mails to Public Relations. In addition to being cautious in dealing with the press, I gave full cooperation to our PR people. If they needed to schedule press contacts on sudden notice, I would do what I could to open a hole in the day's calendar. On the road, I ended up functioning as something of an unofficial traveling press secretary. If there were TV interviews scheduled without someone from GE Public Relations being on hand, I watched the clock to make sure the sometimes aggressive news people didn't turn a five-minute Q&A into a thirty-minute interrogation. Learning well from our PR people, I got pretty good at slipping up behind a cameraman or producer and hissing, "He's got to go . . . he'll be late . . . just one more question . . ."

One of the things I learned about dealing with the press is that it's important to work closely with your PR operation to find a middle ground between being too standoffish and being too eager to get coverage. By keeping the media at arm's length, you lose the chance to tell your side of the story. But if you become addicted to seeing your name in print and your face on TV, it can divert limited time and resources and undermine the number one priority, which is to run a successful business. A scrapbook full of press clippings is no substitute for satisfied customers and a healthy bottom line.

I hope reporters aren't like magicians, who get resentful when you give away their secrets. I'll risk it with one that's as ubiquitous as pulling a rabbit out of a hat. We would get calls late in the day, or late in the week if it was from a weekly magazine, from reporters who would say, "I'm sure Jack wouldn't want to comment, but . . ." He or she would go on to present in brief, general terms the story that was being reported. The implication was that the call was simply a courtesy to let him know what was coming. If I took the bait and agreed that he'd probably not want to comment, the next day we read a story with an anti–Jack Welch twist or one with a source claiming to know what Jack Welch was thinking. If Jack had commented, the context of their story might have changed somewhat. My feeling is that these stories were already written and the reporter didn't want the quote because our input would have messed up his or her spin. Therefore, beware of reporters who are too mellow about *not* getting a comment. It may mean that it's time to turn to the PR people so that they can crank up the sound-bite machine.

HI HO, SIX SIGMA

A chapter on preparedness needs a section on unpreparedness. About the best I can do is admit that I am personally unprepared to chop, kick, and block my way to perfection as a Six Sigma Black Belt.

Alas, not even as a Green Belt (a term given to successful completion of a certain level of a formal training program). Given his role in spreading the gospel of Six Sigma far and wide, for Jack Welch's executive assistant to make that admission is truly scandalous, and only akin to being told that the Lone Ranger's sidekick, Tonto, couldn't ride a horse. But it's true. Jack became such a fan of Six Sigma, a quality management process for reducing errors, that he ordered all exempt salaried employees to be trained in the concept or else kiss your opportunities for promotions good-bye, along with future bonuses and stock options.

The man was serious. So why can't Tonto ride? I was able to get on the horse, and that was deemed good enough. As with many training initiatives, there was a double standard. Jack wanted as many key people exposed to Six Sigma as possible, but he balked at the inconvenience of my being away for the full three days required for the introductory course. The same was true of other members of his leadership team; they didn't want their executive assistants to be gone for three days either.

Since Jack Welch was fond of telling ambitious executives that one way "out of the pile" was to master Six Sigma, we executive assistants on the third floor in Fairfield protested the unfairness of being left out. As a compromise, while our bosses were out of town at a management meeting, a concentrated one-day course was arranged for us, which crammed in all the theories and cut back on the exercises. The session provided enough exposure to Six Sigma concepts and its powerful benefits to allow us to operate in a Six Sigma culture without being clueless about what was happening around us.

And what is Six Sigma? I was afraid you'd ask. I have to assume that while many readers know more than I do about the subject, some do not. A sigma is one standard deviation. Out of one million operations—a million delivered packages, a million light bulbs, or a million hamburgers—statisticians know that most companies average between thirty-five thousand and fifty thousand defects. That's about three sigmas (or roughly 3.5 percent). The higher the number of sigmas, the lower the defect rate. In terms of their safety record, for example, U.S. airlines have a six-sigma rating for safely delivering passengers from one location to another, but get only three sigmas or less for baggage handling and ticketing.

When Jack Welch first embraced the concept after seeing how successful it was in the early 1990s at Motorola and AlliedSignal, GE was doing better than average with a three and a half sigma—in other words, getting it right about ninety-seven out of a hundred times. But that wasn't good enough. Across the company, he wanted six sigmas, or 3.4 defects per million, and he wanted it done in five years. It had taken Motorola eight years to cover the same ground.

The actual work of reducing defects involves close observation and measurement of every step in the process. Identifying the obstacles and clearing them out of the way is carried out with almost religious zeal. And it's no wonder. A cost-benefit analysis done in 1995 showed that by going from three to six sigmas, GE could save from $7 billion to $10 billion. While that's serious money, for a company like GE, which produces medical equipment and jet engines, the lives saved are even more important when you can achieve a 99.99966 percent rate of perfection.[1]

I've never felt seriously handicapped by not taking the three-day course or qualifying for a Green Belt, which required a ten-day training period. I'm also jaded enough to question the utility of a nearly across-the-board training model that takes people away from their jobs for long stretches, when they may never use those skills when they return. The most accurate gauge of whether someone is prepared or unprepared is the ability to do the job well *today*. That's why GE had a bit of a double standard on Six Sigma. While using "or else" to get the attention of the workforce, management wasn't willing to blow away today's results to comply with a strict standard to achieve a future objective. They were willing to accept a reasonable level of unpreparedness, or semipreparedness, in the interest of keeping an orderly process up and running.

In addition, scattered pockets of unpreparedness can be tolerated in the short run, as long as the majority of the workforce is being adequately trained and prepared. Eventually, the bare patches can be backfilled later on.

Beyond Six Sigma, training in other areas of GE isn't quite so pervasive. In fact, if I were used as the standard, the conclusion would be that training is nearly nonexistent. While I was executive assistant to the CEO, I was the classic case of the anybody-but-you candidate for training. It's a problem in many businesses. The busier the employee, the less inclination there is to send her or him away for training. When the course curriculum would come in from our Crotonville education center in Ossining, New York, I'd leaf through it and say, "This looks interesting. Why can't I go?" Jack would shoot back, "You could teach that course," and would walk away.

The irony of my anybody-but-you status was heightened by Jack's history of stomping on anybody-but-you-ism elsewhere. He tied compensation directly to training and was adamant about it. This ended the practice of keeping Tom on the job because he couldn't be spared, while sending Dick to be trained, who was better than Harry but didn't have quite as much talent as Tom. Come bonus time, managers would howl to no avail about how unfair it was for Dick to get a bonus when Tom was the workhorse. A bonus for Tom *and* Dick? No way. Dick did the training and got the bonus. They quickly realized that when Jack said he wanted the best people trained, he meant it.

So where did that leave me? In my case, anybody-but-you-ism was alive and well. However, keep in mind that most training is designed to familiarize the student with policies and processes that he or she does not have experience with. I was totally or marginally immersed in literally every aspect of GE, thanks to my job. It would have been pointless for me to sit through orientations on the workings of the HR review process. I had experienced those subjects for years. While I couldn't have taught the classes, I might have dozed off through a couple of them.

And besides all that, I've had a front-row seat in a fourteen-year training course in advanced business leadership with one hell of a teacher. I can't complain.

Preparedness Takeaways

- By seeing things from someone else's perspective, you'll be better able to anticipate what will be needed in the future.
- Share what you know. This was the centerpiece of Jack Welch's GE. We shared ideas, best practices, and information.
- People who hoard knowledge hurt the company.
- Be ready to improvise.
- Stay on top of current events, not just concerning your company but the international business community. It will help give context to what you do, and it's a good conversation starter.

CHAPTER 10

Adaptability

TO MANAGE UP in this era of rapid and pervasive change means being willing to gracefully and skillfully deal with the unexpected. But that doesn't mean waiting passively for the sky to fall or for fire, flood, and famine to pay a visit. Whatever works means having something to work with. It helps to have an adaptability kit on hand.

Mine consisted of a cell phone, a laptop computer, and what I dubbed my "survival files." I never ventured far from the office without my full kit. If something had happened to the cell phone or the computer, I could have coped. Losing the survival files, however, would have been catastrophic. To me, they were the equivalent of the "football," an attaché case that an aide to the President of the United States carries around with the nuclear missile launch codes inside. Without the survival files, I'd have been unable to arm, aim, and launch Jack Welch.

One of the files held a printout of office, home, and cell phone numbers for all GE officers, advisors, support people, and other key players. This was augmented with the home numbers of their executive assistants, who usually could be counted on to know their manager's whereabouts if the cell phone or home numbers weren't being answered. Let's designate this file Telephone Madness I.

One time there was an emergency and we had to find an executive who was offering career counseling to a colleague but didn't want anybody else in the local office to know about it, so he had arranged the session at an out-of-the-way restaurant. I pried the number out of his executive assistant (she was listed in Telephone Madness I) and called the restaurant. When the headwaiter summoned him to the phone, the manager picked up the receiver and said to me, "So much for a secret meeting! How did you find me here?" He was shocked at the privacy invasion, but I'm sure he was happier that he got that call earlier in the evening, before it was too late for him to act. Weigh what's at stake; if the pluses outnumber the minuses, it doesn't pay to be shy about interrupting.

That same file also held contact information for customers, suppliers, and other GE business partners. There was a section for Welch's family and friends, his doctor, favorite haunts, and the like.

The other file, Telephone Madness II, contained the current calendar and a sheaf of master documents that provided multiple layers of names and emergency numbers, data on who was who and what was what, and an assortment of paperwork showing me how things were supposed to happen (but often didn't) so that I could piece together a resolution to almost any emergency. That file changed from day to day, reflecting what was on the calendar. When Jack Welch was traveling, it could be two or three inches thick. Sometimes it was systematically arranged; more often than not it was a haphazard mess. But the point was that it gave me access to information anytime, anywhere.

I once got a call at home at three o'clock in the morning from Jack, who was returning from an overseas trip and was locked out of his house in Florida. Keys and Jack Welch didn't mix very well. He often lost or forgot them, so I became the official key bearer. If I wasn't around, other arrangements were made. The reason for this three o'clock call was that the arrangements had broken down.

The previous day I had instructed Jack's housekeeper to leave a door open for him, since he would be arriving very early the next morning. After informing Jack of this setup, I brashly—and foolishly—added, "If there's a problem, call me."

And he did. Telephone Madness II saved the day—well, the morning. But there was no saving a good night's sleep. Filed under "Florida," I found what I needed, and tracked down the security number for the complex; someone with a key let him in. If I hadn't brought the file home, I would have had to drive to the office, or he would have had to sleep under a palm tree. Later, the same survival file provided me with the name and number of the housekeeper, who explained that she had left the door from the garage open for him. The problem was, he didn't have any way to get into the locked garage.

While this story underscores the utility of survival files, I realize it also undermines my credibility. My adaptability left Jack Welch unable to adapt. Could he have carried a key with him or memorized a security code? Yes. Could he have found a security person to unlock the door? Yes. But instead he called Connecticut and woke me up—partially, I think, to take a little revenge on me for saying, "If there's a problem, call me."

My colleague, Sue Baye, used to scold me for being an "enabler." And I was. Perversely enough, for all the extra work it spawned, the enabling was a measure of my success at managing up. Sweating the small stuff (like a door key) or pulling an obscure telephone number out of thin air when there was urgent business to conduct is the product of a disciplined attention to detail that Jack came to rely on because it allowed him to focus his attention and energy elsewhere.

To fully appreciate the importance of what I'm trying to get at, it may help if I use the analogy of a sentence that is built around a noun and a verb. Attached to those core elements may be adjectives, adverbs, pronouns, and prepositions—the details. The noun and verb give the sentence its basic meaning and direction; the other components convey nuance, depth, precision, and context. In business, the nouns and verbs properly belong to the person immediately above you, but the other details default to those below who are positioned to manage up. I say default, because details—crucial details—come so fast and furiously these days that they can easily overwhelm any manager who is not supported adequately from below. These details work their way down until someone catches them and manages them back up. If not, important work either doesn't get done, is done in a mediocre way, or strains top management to the breaking point as it struggles to keep up.

Managing up is a form of adaptability that is permeating through all layers of business today because it's the only way to cope with the details that have come to overload the basic noun-verb structure of decision making and its processes. To oversimplify, at one time a GE CEO could say, "Sell light bulbs," and it would have sufficed to give the company its mission. Now, however, the who, where, when, and why—the demographics, inventory turns, financial niceties, and dozens and dozens of other considerations—obscure the noun, *light bulbs*, and the verb, *sell*, beneath a crushing landslide of verbiage, a landslide of details. Picking though the details and making them actionable is a function of managing up.

Be a detail person.

While Jack Welch may have been equipped by temperament and talent to cope with this landslide better than many CEOs of his era, he still needed to trade off one form of adaptability for another. To run a company as immense and diverse as GE, and to run it as hands-on as he did, there wasn't much time for many of the more routine aspects of life. For instance, at some point along the way he lost the ability to shut a refrigerator or cabinet door that he opened, and to turn off a water faucet that he turned on. I would routinely follow him, closing doors and drawers and turning off running water before it overflowed onto the floor. I point this out for a good reason, and not just as payback for the three o'clock call from Florida. He adapted away from what he didn't have to do because there was support available, and adapted toward a focus on higher-yielding priorities.

Yes, he golfed and still had time for a private life. But the business pace was so fast and the pressure so intense that there was an ever-narrowing zone of discretionary activities.

In business today, those of us who manage up must aid and abet a functional adaptation that allows the person one rung above to edit out nonessentials from their life script. Don't overreact to this observation. What I mean is that support staff—and remember, we are all support staff—need to take on more and more responsibility for important functions that are being passed downward in the hierarchy. The process is happening at all levels but is most pronounced at the top, where senior executives are forced to delegate almost all nonessential tasks in order to leave themselves time to deal with the essentials.

And by nonessentials, I'm talking about functions that were once the exclusive property of the big dogs: dealing with major customers, negotiating mergers and acquisitions, and controlling external and internal communications. Where the buck used to stop, the shuck now begins. Not out of dereliction of duty, but as a result of an unavoidable delegation of duty. Do I envision a two-tiered business structure, one tier for those who do nothing but think and another for those who do nothing but drudge work? No. The dividing line will never be that sharp. But there's a trickle-down of functions—some very unglamorous, some extremely fulfilling—that is redefining the workplace. I think it is a situation filled with opportunity for those who are capable of taking responsibility for these functions and demonstrate how skilled and adaptable they are. In that sense, managing up is a means to managing your career up.

A HIGH-SPEED CHASE

I'm just going to pick a figure out of the air that seems intuitively right to me—five. The pace of business is five times faster than when I started my career at GE more than twenty-five years ago. By doing some silly math, like multiplying five times eight hours, I could come up with the contention that one day of work now is the equivalent of one week of work back in 1978. I could be a little off, but I think it's enough to say that things are happening faster and faster. We probably don't need to know how fast.

I blame most of it on computers, e-mail, and cell phones. But I would never give them up—well, maybe the cell phone. That device has managed to make instant communication a reality, or something that's reasonably close to instant. The cell phone has destroyed the "I'll be out of reach" excuse for nearly every businessperson, with the exception of those undergoing major surgery. Within an organization, the cell phone can eliminate troublesome gaps that leave a customer hanging for hours without proper service or put an important deal on hold and in jeopardy when key players can't be located. Armed with the right cell phone numbers, I knew an important message could be immediately sent from Jack Welch to any top or middle-management executive at GE. Some were better than others in promptly responding. There were occasional technical glitches and other valid excuses for a slow callback, but hardly ever anything like the hours that used to be lost as we waited to hear from a wayward executive who hadn't called in for his messages. For every tranquil interlude cut short or destroyed by a ringing cell phone, there is an appreciable uptick in productivity. Taken en masse throughout a company, not to mention the entire world business economy, the productivity gains are enormous.

The speed and reach that cell phones provide can help those who manage up by eliminating the "drying time" that allows problems or complications to harden like chunks of concrete. Those who are managing up need to react quickly, not only to limit potential damage or to seize opportunities, but to stay on top of the ever-expanding to-do list. Cell phones are a blessing in that way.

My personal cell phone curse is the invention of call forwarding. I could—and still do—forward the office-line calls to my cell phone when I step out of the office, which makes me vulnerable to being bombarded with calls in the hallway, the rest room, the elevator, and anywhere else it is maximally inconvenient. Another curse of the new cell phone culture was that since Jack consistently and predictably called me whenever I left the office, I had to carefully time my movements through the dead zone that exists between the Merritt Parkway and my home, a leg that takes about nine minutes. If I wasn't careful, I'd have three calls going to voice mail before I was home or out of the zone on the other side. I adapted by waiting to make the nine-minute run when I knew he was tucked away in a meeting or otherwise unable to phone.

The tyranny of the cell phone also meant that wherever I went I needed to drag along the survival files. A combination cell phone and PalmPilot would have done the trick, but I wasn't adaptable enough to keep such a device updated and the batteries charged.

I used a laptop computer with docking stations at home and the office. One unit for both places meant I wouldn't go crazy updating files or forgetting to transfer them from one machine to another. The advantage of the laptop was that I had access to all the files and all my basic tools at home, like the Rolodex, document files, and e-mail, and therefore didn't have to postpone work I had hoped to finish at the office.

The disadvantage was lugging the computer around, and I know I'm in good company with millions of computer-toting businesspeople. But what's another piece of baggage when I was already schlepping two large duffel bags stuffed full of paper documents, a diaper bag that I'd adapted into a utility carrier, and a purse? Jack always referred to me as the "bag lady" when he saw me coming. All I needed was a shopping cart from the grocery store and a large trash bag filled with empty soda cans to complete the ensemble. Fortunately, I never dropped or lost the laptop. If I had, GE's sophisticated data backup system would probably have come to my rescue. Everything was saved in two or more remote locations in case of a massive power failure or a disaster. It's an arrangement that effectively eliminated the excuse "The computer ate my homework."

Equipped in that way, I could theoretically stay up and running seven days a week, twenty-four hours a day. But I didn't. While there were times like that, mostly the work at home was taking phone calls from Jack Welch, tracking down people he needed to reach, and responding to e-mail, most of which I could do and still enjoy a fairly normal suburban evening and weekend routine.

As you can tell, I surrendered and was taken prisoner in the technology war, a conflict that pits the wired against the unwired. The wired are winning, and that's fine with me. The unwired workplace was a drag. I'll take the hectic, high-speed, megaproductive workplace anytime, even if it means I sleep over the store (my home office is below my bedroom). Like millions of other businesspeople, the last thing I did every night, and still do, is go down there and check my e-mail. Through the windows I hear the rustle of the wind in the trees and the pianissimo water music of the brook that flows into a nearby pond. On the bright screen there might be messages from London, Paris, Tokyo, or New Delhi, both routine questions and urgent reports. Important things are happening, and I'm excited to be part of it.

SPAM AND PIZZA

In Chapter 2, I described myself as an early adapter when it comes to technology, and I am, or was. I'm probably slowing down on mastering the latest high-tech applications like videoconferencing, which takes time to learn. The pace is still too hectic to spare the time, even though the technology would make me more productive in the long run. I confess that I still fax to one recipient at a time, even when there's a group involved and I could use the broadcast function to have the machine dial and send to the entire list. Setting up the broadcast function means stopping, finding the fax instruction manual, and doing the trial-and-error tango. It's easier one at a time.

Maybe I should turn in my early-adapter badge. The fax, however, is becoming obsolete anyway. Compared to ten years ago, it hardly gets used anymore. E-mail rules. Incoming faxes tend to go to the bottom of the pile and get lost. The same goes for ordinary mail, which has become less and less important in the flow of communications. Curiously, in the last few years before Jack Welch retired, the volume of paper mail remained the same but the content seemed to become more and more trivial. Every day the mail room delivered a cart laden with several plastic crates stuffed full of mail; there were hundreds of items. Sue opened and logged all of it, tossed about 50 percent of it, passed on 30 percent to other offices, and handed the last 20 percent to me to be whittled down even more. Probably less than 5 percent of the total ended up on Jack's desk.

A much higher percentage of e-mail made it through the filtering process. Part of the reason is that with regular mail, CEOs and other top executives are not exempted from junk mail, and may actually get more of it than the average person. Then there were autograph hunters, investment touts, people with hard-luck stories asking for money, and a variety of strange characters, like one man who for months kept sending us a dollar every few days for some unfathomable reason. We'd return the cash, a few more days would go by, and back it would come. Sue and I finally gave up and went out for a pizza with the money.

Once Sue answered a call from a man who wanted to know if we had received his message. She asked for his name and typed it into the computer, but there was nothing from him recorded in the mail log. "When did you mail it?" she asked. "Oh, I didn't use mail," he replied. "I sent it telepathically. You should have got it last week." She urged him to try again.

There's plenty of weird e-mail, too, and spam. However, you are spared having to sort it by hand, open the envelopes, and extract the contents. I actually didn't use the delete key all that much except for the spam. What I like about e-mail is how quickly it can be read and processed. To answer a letter, I had to stop what I was doing and draft a formal reply using the proper format, proof it, find the official letterhead, print it, print an envelope, fold the letter properly, stuff the envelope, and seal it. With e-mail I could pull up a standard response that I had used before, modify it to suit the circumstances, and hit the send button.

But I'm making it sound like Jack Welch was not involved with his mail or e-mail. In both cases, he saw everything that went out over his signature. Everything. He took a very dim view of operations that crank out correspondence that seems like it's coming from the person in charge but isn't really. For most letters that went to him, I drafted a proposed response on paper and attached it. Once he okayed the draft, if it was a letter, it was printed out and went back to him in case he wanted to add a handwritten note. For an e-mail, I also composed a draft reply, made any additions he suggested, and hit the send button.

I'm going through all this not because I think it makes for scintillating reading, but to reinforce my contention that managing up is first and foremost the art of saving time for those above you and helping them to prioritize in the face of almost overwhelming demands on their time and attention.

Managing up is first and foremost about saving time.

Jack Welch would have spent hours replying to his mail and e-mail if he had to do it himself. Or, more likely, there would have been no responses at all. Instead, in a matter of minutes he kept abreast of incoming and outgoing correspondence. I probably learned the fine points of handling letters in high school from my business classes. But I had to adapt on my own to the brave new world of e-mail. I quickly realized that if I didn't manage the flow, Jack Welch would be swamped.

Occasionally, I would spot e-mail in his mailbox, and I knew he would stop what he was doing and work on a reply if he saw it. Not that the e-mail was particularly important or urgent, but there would be something about it that was bound to catch his interest. I headed that off by dragging it into my mailbox so that I could gather the information for a reply, which could be moved back into Jack's mailbox once the pace of business slackened enough so that it would be safe to let him at it. Was I overstepping the bounds?

Not at all. I was managing up. There were more important things to be dealt with first. There would have been no such thing as managing up if I had passively given in to the notion that I had no business imposing my judgment on what mail or e-mail went to his desk and what didn't. If I hadn't, there might have been chaos. I wasn't being paid to preside over chaos, and neither was he. By managing up aggressively in this case, my efforts were aimed at helping my boss do his job to the best of his ability.

If I had asked him, "Would you rather be distracted by this e-mail or focus on what's more important?" you and I know what he would have said. At every point in our professional relationship, my actions were out in the open. He always had the option to read the date in the header to see when it arrived and ask, "What are you doing holding this?" And by the way, he occasionally did ask that question. My answer was, "You were busy with other things and I thought it could wait." And that satisfied him every time.

But the real measure of adaptability is not how well you deal with e-mail; it is the ability to adapt to whatever new reality comes along and imposes itself on you and your workplace. Being an early adapter is all well and good, but to be a Jack Welch–style adapter is even better. As hard-charging, independent, and brilliant as he is, he was willing to be managed from below as long as it made him more effective. And that's why I started this chapter by saying that "whatever works" sums up adaptability. Managing up works.

Adaptability Takeaways

- Be an "enabler"—it'll free everyone to do what they do best.

- The details matter.
- Have no shame—get your hands dirty, and be willing to do whatever works to get the job done.
- To get ahead, you've got to master the art of saving time—yours, and that of those above you.
- Trust your judgment, and be prepared to defend it.

CHAPTER 11

Simplicity

IF I SAID I could offer you a set of simple rules for managing up in a company with over three hundred thousand employees and more than twenty operating units, you'd be wise to switch on your BS meter. But don't worry, I'm not going to do that. I'll show you how we dealt with a dynamic and inherently complicated business organization by laying out its major functions on what amounts to the most simple spreadsheet of them all—a calendar. Once that was done, creativity and business savvy were free to make the most of available talent and opportunities.

COUNTING THE DAYS

Our calendar—Jack Welch's calendar—always threatened to take over the operation like HAL in *2001: A Space Odyssey.* We kept CAL at bay, but barely. There are 242 workdays a year. In 1998, to choose one year as an example, we blocked in 166 days with fixed corporate events almost a year in advance. When you spread the remaining 76 open days out across an entire year, that left less than about a day and a half a week unspoken for.

I was CAL's keeper. Around May of every year I would begin to plug dates into a blank calendar. Approximately twenty-nine corporate events were entered, like board meetings, the shareholders' meeting, and holidays. Then there were twenty-eight days of overseas travel for business reviews and other purposes, five days of customer field visits, eleven days of GE Capital Board meetings, ten days of Jack Welch teaching dates at the Crotonville education center, thirteen days of personal commitments (annual medical checks, golf tournaments, etc.), five Business Council days, and ten days of annual commitments to speak to security analysts, attend miscellaneous internal GE Service Council meetings, and the like.

CAL was a monster, but there was room for a little flexibility. Companies are creatures of habit; at least GE was. Certain things happened according to a cycle or season. In our case, an annual leadership meeting for the top operating managers was held the first week in January in Boca Raton, Florida. That's a two-and-a-half-day affair followed by a day of meetings held separately by each unit. Therefore, in January, the first week was spoken for, as was the last week, which was reserved for Jack's annual visit to GE's European businesses. The following fixed pattern of events held throughout the rest of the year:

January: annual operating managers meeting

February: compensation reviews

March/April: Human Resources reviews in the field

May: sales visits to key cities and customers

June: two weeks of GE business and customer reviews
   in Europe

July: strategy reviews

August: vacations and no scheduled meetings

September/October: two to three weeks in Asia

November: budget reviews and update of HR items from
   the spring meeting

December: year-end wrap-up meetings and extended
   holidays

And sprinkled throughout were monthly board meetings, prep sessions, and monthly GE Capital Board meetings.

Everyone understood that there was no arguing with the fixed internal and external dates, but the struggle to get one's preferred time slot with Jack was fierce. Take, for example, the Human Resources reviews, a one-day dive into a GE business's executive talent pool, the object of which was to make sure all the players were capable of swimming in the deep end. Each unit had to present to Jack, the vice chairmen, and our head of HR, Bill Conaty, a full accounting of its personnel strengths and weaknesses, a panoramic picture of how its human resources were being deployed and developed. Jack Welch wanted substance, and he got it. As a result, in terms of planning and execution, those reviews were more than simple one-day events; they preoccupied the unit's leadership for several weeks prior to the review itself.

Consequently, scheduling them was not easy. They were usually in March or April, but the actual dates depended on what was happening out in the field. In other words, if there was an important deal pending or a product rollout, for example, an HR review for that particular unit could be shifted within the two-month window to avoid creating a conflict. These potential conflicts were nearly impossible to predict from Fairfield. I would e-mail key people at the various businesses and ask them to give me a feel for how things were shaping up for that time period. If I was lucky, I'd be given a few dates to consider.

But if I was unlucky—the usual case—I'd have to randomly block in dates, and then all hell would break loose once the calendar was circulated. That's when the great unreported and unseemly chocolate bribery scandal would play out. If every person has a price, mine is chocolate. It became a running gag among the business leadership team that if they wanted to shift their human resources reviews, or any of the other events for that matter, Ro's secret Swiss chocolate bank account was open for business. It was a fun joke, but I got candy sent to me each year by at least one unit that wasn't taking any chances.

Seriously, the juggling could be frustrating. Businesses that were scheduled early in the cycle begged to go later in the month the next year. Some were up to their necks in valid business issues, and others had various scheduling conflicts. If I shifted a date to please one unit, I inconvenienced another. Surprisingly, the back-and-forth was conducted with the utmost civility and good humor. Nobody screamed or pounded the table. There was a tacit understanding that the process was being conducted fairly and that any inconvenience would be shared equally if possible.

Sometimes I had to referee between businesses who wanted the same date. Usually one of them would back off in anticipation that they would receive the same courtesy the next time, when they might need a break even more. Frequently, units would come to the rescue and volunteer to give up a plum date—usually a Wednesday or a Thursday later in the window—figuring that they'd pick up an IOU. This kind of jockeying went on over the entire yearly calendar cycle.

And I wasn't the only one engaged in this massive juggling act. As time went on, two of our best calendar jugglers, Barbara Shoop and Vickie Moran, did the bulk of the individual business lineup. Those four-star jugglers had many long days and restless nights too.

I wish that there had been a way to get this process completed sooner. Four months' lead time was the absolute minimum. I was acutely conscious of how people's lives were intimately and drastically affected by the corporate calendar—CAL could wreck a wedding, a college graduation, or a family reunion. I had a picture in my head of sobbing would-be brides, distraught at their parents' admonition to wait to arrange for the most-in-demand caterer in town until the corporate calendar was issued: "But Daddy, they'll be booked. . . ."

The managing-up lesson is: You can't please everyone, and conflicts are unavoidable. Get used to them.

Conflicts are unavoidable—get used to them.

SHOW AND TELL

As chock-full as Jack Welch's calendar was, sticking to it was more draining for him than it was for anyone else. Take, for example, the July strategy reviews. GE Medical Systems, GE Appliances, or any other business on the schedule for that month only had to prepare for and undergo a one-day session. Jack and a few of his staff had to do more than twenty of them, one right after the other. It was the same for HR reviews, budget reviews, and so on.

What's important to note is the simplicity that's at work here. The individual businesses weren't required to endure weekly or monthly scrutiny. While these sessions—roughly six of them a year per unit—required extensive preparation, there was more than enough time left to manufacture products, provide quality service, and satisfy the customer.

In other words, at GE there was minimal centralization and central planning accompanied by a thin layer of simple, sophisticated controls. The fixed dates and fixed agendas were the means by which Jack checked to see if each business was sticking to the script that was written, for the most part, by that business's own leaders. By keeping the calendar simple in terms of not piling on recurring onerous planning and reporting requirements throughout the year, it was easier to stay focused on the primary mission.

The fact that GE has preserved its tradition of decentralization while growing, at one point, to have the largest market capitalization in the world ($500 billion prior to the 2001–2002 bear market) is testimony to its success. Not only was bigger better, bigger did not smother the unique individuality of its component businesses. And I think the calendar has something to do with it. There was just enough central control and just enough freedom to cultivate entrepreneurship and yet give it the kind of momentum and muscle that comes from a large corporation.

CONSENSUS BUILDING

With our corporate calendar in place, there were still seventy-six open days left on Jack's calendar, some of which were used for meetings involving several individuals. Contrary to the public image of CEOs as autocrats, Jack Welch didn't just order his people to drop everything and report to Fairfield. Why not? You can't run successful businesses that way. It's way too inflexible.

Scheduling open days was easier than blocking out an entire year—a bit. I'll start with what I didn't do.

I didn't call each one of the participants and ask what days they had available. I'm pretty quick to pick up a phone, but that approach would have eaten up an hour or more, depending on how many people were involved. Also, it would have left me as the go-between from then on: Joe can't do Tuesday but he can make it on Thursday. Can Jill do Thursday? Multiply that scenario by the number of participants and my initial investment of time would have escalated massively.

Instead, I composed a simple meeting grid that listed the names of the participants down the left-hand margin and displayed proposed dates across the top. The dates were drawn to accommodate Jack's schedule and perhaps one or two others who were considered indispensable to the meeting. I'd fax out the grid and request each person to mark a date or two to indicate when they could attend.

When I got them back from each person, I did a master grid that looked like this:

	6/10	6/27	6/28	7/1	7/15	7/16
Jenson		X	X	X		
Atkins	X		X	X		
Cooper				X		X
Kincaid		X	X			
Warner		X	X	X		
Ellis	X					
Lukens			X	X		
Cantor	X		X		X	
Hammond	X					X

The two most popular dates were June 28 and July 1 (which probably wouldn't happen in real life, since July 1 is crowding up against the Independence Day holiday). I would then send another grid out with those two dates and ask for choices again. The second time around, Ellis and Hammond, seeing how the consensus was emerging, might take a second look at their calendars and free themselves up for either June 28 or July 1. Whichever date got the most votes would be selected for the meeting. I'd e-mail out the results, and usually only one, maybe two, of the participants would find it impossible to attend on that date.

As simple and seemingly trivial as the grid appears, it's a useful tool for those who are managing up. One of the forgotten aspects of management is the importance of lateral management. The names in the left-hand column of the grid are on the same team; they are peers. An effective organization recognizes that peer-to-peer interactions need to run smoothly. The grid, as a managing-up tool, helps take some of the potential bumps out of that process. By keeping simplicity in mind, squabbling over meeting dates and wasting time and energy on scheduling issues are kept to a minimum.

TIME OFF FOR GOOD BEHAVIOR

And now for the last of the calendar vis-à-vis simplicity. You may have noticed that August would have no meetings scheduled. August is when Jack Welch used to take his vacation every year. What's simple and effective about this was instead of pretending that GE was up and running full blast in August, the company went into vacation mode. The doors were open, the lights were on, services were provided to customers, but things slowed appreciably.

No edict was issued to the effect that people had to take their vacations in August. Rather, it evolved in reaction to Jack's policy of spending time away from the office, and other executives followed suit. Getting many of the players on the same schedule—a European schedule, I might add, since many of GE's operations are global—made it easier to plan and conduct business during the rest of the year. Another benefit was that by taking a break, Jack was offering an example to others who might have been prone to workaholism. Dedication is fine, but there's no sin in resting and recharging your batteries. August vacations also do help curb the two-vacation syndrome: one vacation taken in the office while nothing is really happening, and another later in the year when things are hopping.

SMALL WORLD

It was my embrace of simplicity that enabled me to stay on top of my job at all times. But it was also Jack's insistence on simplicity that made my job so demanding, thanks to his decision to keep the CEO's office staff to two people—Sue and me. Many large corporations have six, seven, or more employees handling the workload.

Less is sometimes more.

I'm not going to argue that less is more. Less worked for Jack Welch, and that was all that really mattered. In dealing with other corporations, I often wondered how their larger CEO staffs were able to stay coordinated and avoid communications breakdowns. At one point we added a third person, but due to the configuration of the office, she had to sit outside the main work area. That was just enough isolation to leave her out of the flow of activities and deprive her of what she needed to know to make a contribution. As a result, she was forced to refer calls and questions to me. In turn, I didn't have a chance to get her up to speed and keep her there. In the end, it made more sense to go back to two people.

By keeping his immediate staff lean, Jack Welch avoided bureaucratizing himself. Mail was delegated to Sue, the rest to me. And he is such a genius at delegation that once responsibility was assigned, he didn't want to hear any more about it. If I had announced that I was going to divvy much of what I was handling among a hundred people, it wouldn't have fazed him—so long as the work got done.

Managing-down skills are necessary. The managing-up–managing-down linkage works best when it is kept as simple as possible. If not, the complexity may work against managing up effectively. I don't think it is an insurmountable obstacle, however. The top executives in each of GE's operating units managed up in their relationship with Jack Welch while delegating downward into large, diverse organizations. They fulfilled their commitments to GE and to their boss.

We had another effective technique for achieving simplicity. To paraphrase Shakespeare—"The first thing we do, let's kill all the lawyers"[1]—I say, first shred the useless paper and then we won't need to kill the lawyers.

As a rule, if Jack Welch wasn't going to need a document again, it went into the shredder or was shipped to another office.

GE must comply with a federal law, the Hart-Scott-Rodino Act, that mandates a high level of documentation when acquisitions are made and requires GE lawyers to assemble the documents that are in the possession of the people involved in the deal. In other words, if that material is in your files the lawyers have to look at it at some point, no matter if it duplicates material they already have. GE Capital, for example, invests in hundreds of businesses. Each time a deal was proposed to the board, of which Jack was a member, a briefing book filled with documents was handed to him and the other members. When he came back to the office with the paperwork, we'd hold on to it for twenty-four hours or so and then it would hit the shredder.

The last thing we needed to have was the GE lawyers rummaging through our files every other day gathering Hart-Scott-Rodino material. It still existed unshredded elsewhere; it just wasn't in our office. So when I got a call from a conscientious member of our legal department asking, "What do you have in the files on . . . ?" I could truthfully answer, "Nothing."

Simplicity Takeaways

- You can't please everyone—get used to it.
- Make paper your enemy—toss it, shred it, or ship it to storage, but get it out of your office.
- Less is *sometimes* more.

CHAPTER 12

Fairness

YOU PROBABLY DON'T want to read about all the nice, fair things I did over the course of my career at GE, or what a fair guy Jack Welch is. Therefore, I'm going to plunge straight into a brief examination of how Jack handled the ultimate test of fairness—rewarding those who succeeded and dealing with those who didn't.

Jack's principal fairness tool was the "vitality curve." It was a bell curve that placed GE employees in three categories: the top twenty, the vital seventy, and the bottom ten. If it seems overly statistical—bear with me. The curve is a model of a valid statistical assumption that an organization's best performers will amount to 20 percent of its workforce; the next slice, midrange workers— many of whom have promise but have room for development—

accounts for 70 percent; and finally, the remaining 10 percent, who are performing poorly and show no likelihood of improving, end up in the third grouping.

It's as simple as ABC. The A's are rewarded handsomely, the B's are encouraged to grow and become A's, and the C's leave the company. The easy way to rank or make these differentiations would be with a computer. Key in sets of numbers that attempt to quantify performance, push a button, and the stars are born and the losers shorn.

Simple—and hugely unfair. Every year, Jack Welch spent a full day—and a long one at that—with each of the more than 20 GE operating units, closely scrutinizing and evaluating their staff. Earlier in the book I noted Jack's penchant for rapid-fire questions and his ability to listen hard to the answers. At those sessions he fired off burst after burst:

What are your plans for Gillespie?

What are his strengths?

What are his weaknesses?

Has he grown enough in his current position?

Does he show enough passion?

What are his values?

Jack Welch's role in these sessions, however, was secondary. The primary goal was to require the operating units to undertake a rigorous analysis of their workforce, make it an organic part of their business strategy, and be held accountable for its success. His presence reinforced the importance of the process, established that the CEO would take a dim view of "cooking" the evaluations, and kept him fully informed as to the depth and quality of GE's talent pool.

Jack regarded nondifferentiation as the height of unfairness. "Differentiation," as it came to be known, was a way to reward the A players with promotion bonuses and stock options, develop members of the B group to broaden and deepen their contribution, and eliminate the C group, who put a drag on the company (and on those in groups A and B). Treating all employees equally is unfair when some are making a significantly greater effort and impact on a company's success. It is a sure way to demoralize your stars and drive them to look for a different place to work.

Treating all employees equally is unfair to your star performers.

Jack Welch didn't mince words when it came to making the tough decisions as to who would stay and who would go. He made it clear to managers that if they couldn't bring themselves to differentiate, they were themselves candidates for the C group. And that tended to get their attention. By taking such a proactive role in the process—in effect, forcing it—Jack kept it fair and aboveboard. His involvement meant that it would not and could not be ignored. Nor was "don't like her/do like him" favoritism or unfairness tolerated toward the C group. Their substandard performance had to be documented and not based just on someone's unsubstantiated opinion.

For those who are managing up while simultaneously managing down, you have to make the hard decisions on rewarding and penalizing members of your team. Taking action against poor performance is not a pleasant task. But it does the person above and everyone else no service when you avoid seeing to it that your team is as strong as possible. A conscientious gardener pulls the weeds so that the cash crop will grow and prosper, and he prunes back the deadwood from his trees. Ducking these chores sabotages your own best interest, and it isn't fair to your team or the person above.

TEACHER AND GUIDANCE COUNSELOR

There's no single title, like *differentiation*, to describe Jack Welch's technique for intervening in an operation that was experiencing trouble or not living up to expectations. Consequently, I've dubbed it "assigning extra homework." (Although homework was often a feature of "deep dives," Jack's name for the pet projects he adopted over the years. Even so, it was a stand-alone concept.)

About once a year, maybe twice, Jack would run across a GE unit that needed something extra to get it back on track or to realize its full potential. The extra turned out to be nudging, coaching, and hand-holding from the CEO himself. Jack has told me—he's told a lot of people—that he saw his role at GE as that of a teacher. He liked nothing better than helping people grow.

Extra homework was a way to force growth and ensure that it continued without necessitating micromanagement or imposing drastic solutions like personnel changes. First, Jack would bear down on the operation that had caught his attention, employing personal visits, phone calls, e-mails, and faxes full of questions and Socratic guidance (instructions phrased like questions: "Do you think we need to triple-check this?"). Typically, he'd push the leaders of the business to set tangible goals and come up with a plan of action to achieve them.

But these weren't planning exercises. Jack wanted to see results. He would require his "students" to report back to him once a week or so, usually on a Friday, with the results they had achieved. Sometimes they were praised for their efforts; sometimes they were encouraged to do better. This simple procedure was a way to energize and focus an operation. Every Monday morning, they knew that in less than five days they would be on the CEO's radar screen and held accountable for what they did and didn't achieve.

In turn, Teacher Welch had something to work with as a learning tool and as a yardstick to measure progress. He knew that without the extra homework, the unit would probably soon revert to business as usual, the objectives would not be met, and the problems would be left unresolved. And this is where fairness came into play. Better to do homework and have direct help from the CEO than to endure failure and recriminations. Jack was using his time and resources by functioning as an in-house superconsultant. The most famous example of homework was when he intervened with GE Medical Systems to increase the life of the tubes in the CT scanning machines from 25,000 hours to more than 100,000. Jack turned the assignment over to Marc Onetto and had him handing in weekly extra homework assignments for four years. Onetto, a Frenchman, would get notes like this one back from the teacher: "Too slow, too French, move faster or else." Of course, there were also notes praising Onetto and his operation for the progress they were making.[1]

After five years, Jack's students overshot their target by 100 percent—producing tubes that lasted more than 200,000 hours, a 400 percent improvement over the old 25,000-hour lifetime.

Was it the result of extra homework or extra attention from the teacher? Probably a little of both.

The extra homework assignments were a way for Jack Welch to manage down. But Marc Onetto was in the enviable position of having the undivided attention of his boss at least once a week for four years. I have to believe that Marc had some time to spare for managing up or, at the very least, to avail himself of Jack's special skills to deal with special problems. For example, Onetto almost lost his chief engineer in the middle of the project, which would have been a major setback, but Jack weighed in and talked the man into staying. Without the ongoing teacher-student relationship with Onetto, who's to say what might or might not have happened?

Nonetheless, the dynamic did create a managing-up opportunity in that it provided valuable access to Jack Welch. Instead of waiting for your boss to manage down by assigning extra homework, take a more proactive managing-up stance. By establishing an active and regular line of communication with the person above to seek advice, report on new developments, and ask for help, you can replicate many of the extraordinary benefits of extra homework.

MAGIC WORDS

Two important functions of a leader are to offer a concrete definition of business reality—a 100,000-hour-life CT scan tube or else—and to say thank you. A day rarely went by when Jack Welch didn't do both. By repeatedly hammering home fundamental messages like "idea sharing," "the boundaryless organization," and "number one or number two—fix, sell, or close," he not only defined reality, he created it. Obviously this is good communications—which I'll discuss in the next chapter—but foremost, I see it as pure, practical fairness. Mixed messages and shifting targets are unfair. They leave a business and its people adrift.[2]

- Can you do your best without knowing how your boss defines "best"?
- How can you be sure today's hard work won't be made irrelevant by tomorrow's erratic shift in priorities?
- Are the personal sacrifices worth it when nobody seems to notice or care?

Much of what Jack did on a daily basis was calculated to provide positive, reassuring, and inspirational answers to those kinds of questions. I'd estimate that thousands of handwritten notes went out over the twenty years he served as GE's chairman and CEO. It was his way of defining reality, showing that he cared about an individual's contribution and sacrifice, and saying thank you.

In an important way, the medium was the message. Jack didn't like formal recognition ceremonies, plaques, or handing out (or receiving) knickknacks. He spent only a tiny fraction of his time on the ceremonial aspects of his job. He could have jetted around the country and around the world taking credit for GE largesse or giving people pats on the back. Not his style, though. In going through the newspapers or reviewing public relations material, when he spotted photographs of a corporate staff representative handing over a check to charity or the like, he would flag it and let it be known that the individual involved had no business taking the limelight away from the local business unit that had a direct relationship with the charity. He wanted a personal touch, not a PR "opportunity."

I had standing instructions dating back fourteen years to remind him—nag him, if necessary—to write out brief notes on his embossed card stock stationery to say thank you for everything from White House state dinners to invitations to play in charity golf tournaments or speak at college campuses. I well remember the White House state dinner because, being new on the job in 1989, I neglected to make sure that Jack sent out a thank-you note to George and Barbara Bush the very next morning after the dinner—an oversight (only one day late) that drew a testy "You're supposed to remind me about things like this." And believe me, I've been reminding him promptly ever since.

The other variety of thank-you note usually went to GE employees. It was handwritten on an eight-by-ten sheet of white bond with a cheap black felt-tip pen. Those were the "atta boys" and the "naughty boys"—the "you did great" and the "you can do better" notes. On most days that Jack was in the office, we faxed out a small stack of them around the country and overseas. People loved to get them and, surprisingly, even saved the "naughty boys." Many of these "atta boy" notes are framed on desks and office walls of employees and nonemployees around the world. A personal note signed by Jack Welch was like having a baseball card signed by Willie Mays. And to reassure autograph collectors: They are all authentic. On person-to-person communications, Jack felt that a signature was a gesture similar to a handshake—strictly do-it-yourself.

He carried this attitude over to incoming mail, as well. Anonymous letters were tossed, unless they were from GE people who had a legitimate fear of retaliation for reporting abuse or lapses. In those cases, I'd pass the letter on to the business unit that was involved along with instructions to check out the situation and report back. Otherwise, anonymous letters never reached Jack's desk. Neither did unsigned Christmas cards. He hated the kind that came with the name of the sender preprinted. They all went into the wastebasket.

We processed, I should note, about 550 Christmas cards every year. Each one went out with his signature, and most had short handwritten messages, too. I have to share with you Jack's attitude toward receiving tokens of recognition and appreciation. I should probably consult the Guinness Book of Records before I say this, but I'll live dangerously: Jack Welch has one of the largest collections of crystal pyramids in the solar system. I've often wondered if UFOs use them as a navigation aid along the East Coast of the United States.

For whatever reason, crystal pyramids are very popular gifts, and while Jack Welch was greatly honored by the gestures, they all wound up in a storage space in the Fairfield headquarters that we dubbed "the gift closet." As of this writing, the gift closet is still packed full of crystal pyramids and other items, since Jack and

I were clever enough to "forget" to clean it out when he retired and moved to a new office several miles away. Sue Baye, who is still working in the CEO's office, has called me a couple of times about emptying the closet and I've promised to make it a top priority . . . eventually.

I know I'm making Jack sound ungrateful, but he was genuinely appreciative of all the honors he received. He just wasn't a knickknack and plaque kind of guy. His office was decorated sparsely. There were some family photos (all the grandchildren), photographs of Presidents Clinton and Bush (I and II), and a few others. No plaques, no trophies, no Revere bowls, and no pyramids. The gift closet helped us keep the mementos from filling every inch of wall and shelf space and then spreading to adjoining offices and hallways until the entire third floor was covered with Jack Welch treasure and tribute like King Tut's tomb. And there were also two other purposes to the closet: It spared us from having to confront the question of what was to be done with the stuff—a pawnshop? A donation to the Metropolitan Museum of Art? I don't think so. The final purpose of the closet is best conveyed by a practical question, "What became of that crystal pyramid we gave you in 1992?"

The closet was our "just in case" insurance. I can't remember ever actually rushing to redecorate Jack's office because of an impending visit. But a panicky office redecoration was always a possibility. We had a large—twenty-four by thirty-six—framed photograph of a Saudi businessman stashed away in the closet. It had been sent to Jack to commemorate a meeting they once had. Occasionally, I asked him if we could get rid of it, and he'd say, "Better not. What if he stops by?" I resisted the temptation to ask, "Do you think he'd really fall for that? An office decorated with only a few family photos, a couple of presidents, and on one wall a single photo of a Saudi businessman?"

THE WOMEN OF GE

I referred to Jack's "atta boy" and "naughty boy" notes a few pages ago. What about the "atta girl" notes? Sooner or later, I have to face the issue of GE's image as a place where men rise to the top jobs and women hit the glass ceiling. A chapter on fairness is a good place to address it.

When I started with the company in 1978, I worked for a woman, the head of the legal department's law library. But that was unusual. The typical boss at the time was a man in his late forties or fifties. The handful of women who were in supervisory positions tended to be at lower levels and mostly in support functions.

That was the old GE. The new GE under Jack Welch gradually opened up more management opportunities for women. But the record was mixed. In the first half of Jack's twenty-year tenure, the pace of advancement was more glacial than gradual. While more women trickled into executive positions, the numbers were still relatively paltry compared to male executives. Jack had a full plate during this period. He was busy reinventing GE, taking the company through traumatic downsizing and a burst of unprecedented change. Helping more women climb the ladder was not one of his initial priorities, and he acknowledged it.

Another reason for the slow pace was the nature of GE's businesses. The core of the company was still heavy manufacturing, from locomotives and nuclear power plants to refrigerators and light bulbs. An engineering degree was the ticket, and not many women engineers were graduating from universities in the 1960s and '70s.

In the second half of Jack's run as CEO, things were different. The new emphasis on services attracted experienced, well-credentialed women, including those with engineering degrees. They were now in the job pipeline, and diversity in the marketplace was creating competitive pressure for an equally diverse workplace. While the crown jewels of the company—businesses such as Medical Systems, Aircraft Engines, Plastics, and Power Systems—were run by men, sizable operations, including Fleet Services and Information Systems, had women in the top jobs. Ironically for these women executives, being part of the larger GE family meant that they did not get the public and news media recognition they would have had for leading stand-alone companies of the same or even smaller size.

Early in my career, I worked on preparing human resources briefing books that tracked up-and-coming executive talent. Out of a couple of hundred rising stars, there would be only three or four women. In my last five years working in the CEO's office, those briefing books featured thirty or more women, or about 20 percent of the fast-track executive talent pool. We were doing better, but still had a way to go to bring the number up to a more appropriate level.

The "guys" at GE knew this and did their best to rectify the imbalance, but refused to simply hire women for the sake of meeting quotas. One of Jack's major legacies was his choice of Jeffrey Immelt as CEO and chairman. Jeff is determined to move more qualified women and minorities up the executive ladder.

I did my part to sensitize Jeff and some of the other executives. And this story demonstrates that managing up comes in many forms.

When it came time for annual strategy reviews, I'd stand by Jack's conference room door as a business unit's team of executives entered to make their presentation. If it was an all-male lineup—as it often was—I'd ask as they passed by, "Where are the women? Are they still downstairs?" I'd make a big show of turning and looking behind them for stragglers, knowing full well that when I finally shut the door behind the last man to arrive there wouldn't be a single pair of X chromosomes in the room.

They were really sheepish about it. I did my number once on Jeff Immelt when he ran Medical Systems. "Where are the women, Jeff? Parking the cars?"

He turned and said, "Rosanne, I promise you when this team comes back in five months, I'll have three women on it."

"Want to bet?" I asked. He accepted the challenge and agreed to take me to dinner if three women weren't part of the team next time. I assumed that he was in the process of interviewing and hiring the three or else he wouldn't have been so bold.

Five months later, Jeff's team appeared—with two women on it. "I believe you owe me dinner," I said. One of his candidates had dropped out in the last phases of the hiring process, he explained. While he got credit for the two, a bet's a bet. Jeff has yet to pay up, but he will. It's only fair.

Fairness Takeaways

- Not every employee deserves to be treated equally—to do so is to demoralize the stars of your company.
- Get comfortable with separating the wheat from the chaff, and let go of the chaff.
- The higher up on the totem pole you are, the better teacher you need to be.
- Offer second, third, and fourth chances. But take a closer look if you are nearing a fifth.
- Firmly define your targets and your message.

CHAPTER 13

Communication

JACK WELCH was a backseat flyer. He'd sit at the small conference table in the front cabin of the company's aircraft reviewing reports and signing documents as intently as if he was still in the office rather than cruising at thirty thousand feet. But every now and then, Jack would look up to check a panel of instruments on the forward bulkhead that displayed the airspeed, altitude, and time to the destination. "What are you trying to do, save gas?" he'd call out toward the open cockpit door. "Step on it!"

If the flight was bumpy, he'd grouse about it and order the pilots to hunt around for a smoother ride at another altitude: "Can't you pull this thing up?" Or, noticing that we were running ahead of schedule and would arrive early, he'd yell, "What's the hurry?" After close to nearly twenty years of that kind of kibitzing, the flight crew just went about their business and flew the plane the way they saw fit—safely. Jack, for his part, would go back to his reading until he was inspired by another shake, rattle, or roll to issue more edicts, and he kept it up until the wheels touched down.

I realize that the term *paradigm*, so overused in the early 1990s, is now out of fashion, but this story captures the essence of the Welch communications paradigm. When it came to communications, he believed that there was no such thing as too much of it. To run the company, he became a virtual human megaphone.

From the day he took over as CEO, Jack let loose with a steady stream of words, millions of them over the years. He coached and counseled, strategized, talked tactics, taught, and tested ideas. When he walked on board that airplane there was no way he could turn off the flow and sit there quietly. His car trips were the same way. Our limo drivers were subjected to "Why did you turn there?" "This isn't the best route across town," and "What are you doing in the left lane?" Since his retirement, I have been pressed into service occasionally to drive him somewhere, and more than once after repeated critiques of my driving technique I pulled to the side of the road and asked him to get out. "If I'm such a lousy driver, go right over there to the pay phone and call a cab," I remember once saying (to no effect whatsoever).

Jack's backseat driving and flying are by-products of a multilayered communications model that employed almost every medium to broadcast his messages into all the nooks and crannies of GE. And yet communications was never allowed to become an end unto itself, as it can in some companies that are great at cultivating an image and highlighting a message, but in the process neglect the basics of business. Running the company—not talking about it—was Jack's primary mission. In the early 1990s, when GE was first starting to be held out as a model corporation for the new era, he received several speaking requests each month from various organizations, many of them headed by people Jack knew well. I'd hear him on the phone turning them down. "Sorry, I can't do it. I have a company to run," he would say.

He might just as easily have said, "Sorry, I can't do it. I have a company to communicate with." Think of the communications model as being shaped like a pyramid. At the top was an occasional formal speaking engagement, like the keynote to the annual shareholders' meeting and a few other major venues. In the next layer down were contacts with Wall Street analysts laying out the company's plans and prospects, and below that were interviews with the news media. As the pyramid's base widened there was a major stratum of informal question-and-answer sessions with GE employees and outside groups; underneath that were teaching sessions at the Crotonville education facility. Finally, at the base itself, was one-on-one give-and-take with GE's business leaders by phone, e-mail, and in person throughout each day.

By turning the pyramid upside down to balance on its apex (imagine a funnel), you'll have a good view of the way Jack's torrent of words flowed from his highest-priority audience—GE's top executives—through the other layers and became more refined and concentrated as it cascaded lower. By devoting the bulk of his communications efforts at the base and midsection of the pyramid, Jack Welch was running the company by relentlessly keeping his primary audiences both on message (change, service, idea sharing, etc.) and on target (growth and profits). He converted communications from being just another management tool into the engine that propelled the company forward. And by taking the message and the target to the secondary audience—analysts, the press, the business community, and the public—with flair and informality, he created a context for success, which might even be more accurately called an expectation for success, that added immensely to GE's value.

> ## Communication is more than
> ## just a tool—it is a catalyst.

As I watched this take place—and, yes, took part in it—I was struck by how practical and tactical the communication always was. Through example, Jack taught GE employees to ask themselves and their colleagues simple questions: "What are we doing right? What are we doing wrong? What can we do better?" It provoked a running dialogue that spread throughout the company, making it more freewheeling, interactive, and open to new ideas. Idea sharing, one of his mantras, would have been impossible without a culture of communications.

No one was excluded from that culture, not even organized labor, which in many other companies is treated like an alien presence or something that's not quite part of the family. Union leaders had full and regular access to Jack Welch. For example, GE Appliances, based in Louisville, Kentucky, had one of the largest union shops in the company. When Jack visited Louisville for the annual spring HR review, lunch was always reserved for a get-together with local union leaders. It was an opportunity to communicate face-to-face. Jack enjoyed interacting with that group of people because they were real—the guys next door who could tell him more about the state of a business in a thirty-minute lunch than in four hours of charts and presentations.

There was no agenda, just a free-flowing discussion. If the union people had a gripe, they talked it through. And if Jack had something he needed to put on the table, he did. Mostly, he wanted to listen, and that willingness to hear what the other guys had to say was probably the key to a little-noted fact about labor and GE: In the twenty years that Jack Welch served as CEO, the company did not have a single major strike.

Those lunches were a safety valve. Instead of talking only when there was a contract being negotiated or because of a dispute, both sides established a working, nonconfrontational relationship that was there when it was needed to head off a potential crisis. What's more, the frequent meetings helped the union understand where Jack Welch was coming from, and vice versa. As a result, they all ended up at the same goal line: a successful company that provided well-paying jobs.

WORDWORKS AND WATERWORKS

Much of what I did in terms of managing up was to function as the dam keeper. I regulated the flow of several (but not all) of the main streams of communications to and from Jack Welch. My job was to serve as a human floodgate. The purpose wasn't to block what came over the dam or through its sluices but to direct the flow so that it could be processed and put to work in the most useful ways. Just as a real dam keeper releases only enough water to allow the power generators to operate at peak capacity, and to maintain the downstream flow within its banks without flooding, my goal was to keep the flow from rising to a dangerous level that could wash out productivity and sound decision making.

Dangerous was a backlog of several hundred e-mails that had not yet been dealt with and another hundred or so new ones from that day. Dangerous was also a phone list of more than one page. With hundreds of e-mails and calls a day, a larger backlog would have meant that important messages were at greater risk of being lost in the flood. At the end of the day, I could go home with something approaching peace of mind if I was under two hundred pending e-mails. They had all been opened and read, however. I just needed more information or a chance to run a proposed answer by Jack to bring them to closure. On the phone calls that came in, I

kept a sheet of paper on his desk with a terse, one- or two-line nota-
tion of the date, the time, the name, the message, and either a quick
background summary to give context to the message or a "let's discuss" note. Rather than take the time to write—and force him to
read—a long explanation, it was often quicker to give him a verbal
briefing on what the caller had told me or what I had already done
to follow up. I admit to being a phone list drill sergeant. I pushed
hard to have the calls disposed of before I was ever forced to make
a second sheet.

Keeping the call list short had three purposes. One, it served
as an early warning system. As it got longer, it told me that our
response time was lagging. Two, it spared me from having to prioritize calls into A, B, and C categories. With a short list, he could
quickly run his eyes down the page and pick out the most important ones that required immediate callbacks. And three, it was one
less thing that I needed to hassle him about—which brings me
back to nagging.

**Nagging or persistence means not dropping
the subject until it is resolved.**

As far as I'm concerned, nagging is a special and important
communications skill for those who manage up. You may use
another term, if you prefer. "Making suggestions," "being persistent," "offering timely reminders," or "nudging" would do just as
well, but whatever it's called, it amounts to not dropping the subject
until some form of resolution occurs. To manage up effectively, you
need to be brave enough to persist; otherwise the issue will remain
open. It doesn't pay to take the easy way out by moving on to new
business, especially if the old business is the kind that gets nastier
and messier the longer it awaits action. I knew that Jack wasn't a

procrastinator or one to avoid troublesome issues, which made it easier for me to "remind" him when he had probably overlooked an item in the rush of business.

Being persistent, however, doesn't mean that you have to make yourself a pain in the neck. Good timing is important. Many small chores get put aside precisely because they are small. Save them for times when the pressure is off and major items are not the focus of attention. If the timing and circumstances aren't right, don't force it. A light touch and a sense of humor help, too. After Jack published his memoirs, instead of harping at him to autograph copies for friends and colleagues, I'd pile the books on his desk so that he had to sign them just to clear the space. At times the desk looked like one of those table displays at the front of Barnes & Noble. He knew exactly what I was doing and why I was doing it.

Fortunately, Jack never told me to stop bugging him. In fact, that possibility worried me less than hearing "Why didn't you remind me?" or "You should have told me about this and I would have taken care of it." If you don't like the idea of being a nag, keep in mind the consequences of *not* nagging.

WAVING THE FLAG

At GE, one of the consequences of not being nagged by Rosanne was being nagged by Jack. I'm shifting focus a bit here to extend what's clearly a managing-up function into its managing-down incarnation. As CEO, Jack Welch nagged his subordinates—only it was called coaching, leading, and motivating. He never let up until his teams brought the pending issue to closure. He pushed, pulled, and prodded.

Occasionally, I nagged so that he wouldn't have to, and to spare someone from being subjected to nagging à la Welch. In fourteen years, it probably happened once or twice a year: I'd notice something amiss around headquarters that if it came to his attention would become a major flap. To head off problems, I provided a little preemptive constructive criticism at the risk of seeming to be throwing my weight around.

One Memorial Day, I made the mistake of turning into the main gate to the Fairfield complex and noticing that the U.S. flag wasn't displayed. I had just driven past a classic New England village green that was all decked out with flags and bunting, and filling up with townspeople preparing for the annual parade. The sight made me feel both patriotic and testy—testy because it was a beautiful day and I was headed for the office. As I rolled up to the security booth, I stuck my head out of the car window and said to the guard, "Is there any reason why there isn't a flag up on that pole? This is Memorial Day, you know."

And so began the five-day fuss over the flag. (It may only have lasted three days, but it seemed longer.) My question drew such a look of dismay from the guard, I wondered if I had run over his foot. He assured me that the flag would be raised immediately. I drove on but could see the man in the rearview mirror rushing around to get the Stars and Stripes up the pole.

Later, mostly out of pure curiosity, I asked Dan Arenovski, the manager who was in charge of security for the building, if there was a policy reason why the flag would be up on certain days and not others. Could it have been because it was a holiday or a long weekend? No, he said, the flag was supposed to be raised every morning. He must have subsequently mentioned the oversight to the guard—probably something casual like "Hey, did you remember to hoist the flag this morning?" That drew a bunch of excuses, including "It was raining," and degenerated into buck passing— the guard on the previous shift had gotten off at six o'clock and should have raised the flag at dawn, before the shift changed. It became a tempest in the security department's coffeepot. The upshot was that a new checklist of duties was issued that included mandatory flag raising and lowering.

I could have kicked myself for opening my big mouth and making myself public enemy number one with the guard staff. Every time I drove through the gate from then on, I imagined hearing them mutter, "There goes the flag nag." On the plus side, the incident brought attention to the importance of displaying the flag, and I bet they haven't missed a day since.

RUMOR HAS IT . . .

Out of all the business books on communications that have been written, not one has addressed the question of how the word is spread throughout an organization like GE concerning hugely important subjects such as the CEO's preference for certain brands of diet soda, flavors of frozen yogurt, or taste in colors of the hallway. And I'm about to fill that void.

First, though, by way of background I have to tell a story about an emotionally troubled lady who persisted in calling one of my colleagues at NBC to complain that the television network was pointing its array of satellite dishes and antennas at her New York City apartment to eavesdrop. My colleague's polite denials went in one ear and out the other. Based on the version of the story I've heard, she finally asked the woman for her address and told her to hang on a moment. After a minute or two she went back on the line and said, "You know, you're right. By mistake someone pointed our gear right at your apartment. I've had it redirected somewhere else, so there's nothing to worry about. Please accept our apologies." The caller thanked her, hung up, and that was the last we heard from her.

My explanation for the spread of Jack Welch trivia throughout GE is that NBC's satellite dishes and antennas were redirected away from that lady's apartment and aimed at GE's headquarters, and that's how a rumor circulated that Jack hated Diet Pepsi and banned it from ever being served in the headquarters building. It's the only possible explanation for the silly myths of that sort that popped up from time to time. I bet he was asked once what he wanted to drink with his turkey sandwich (a favorite, and that's no legend) and he said, "A diet Slice." In seconds, the NBC supersnoops were saying, "Aha, he hates Diet Pepsi . . . get the word out!"

Since many of us seem to have lost our sense of humor these days, judging by a spate of lawsuits against satirical writers, I should point out that I'm kidding about the Diet Pepsi rumormongers, and so was my colleague when she "confessed" to the nutty caller about the network's eavesdropping. There really is no satisfactory explanation as to how these trivial and usually wildly inaccurate stories spread other than the old standby that tales are garbled beyond recognition as they are passed from person to person.

I got a call once from a GE staff member who said, "I understand that Jack Welch hates the new hallway carpeting." Huh? They were all set to tear up perfectly serviceable carpeting on the strength of a wild rumor or, worse, a false report put out to cover someone's tracks who really did despise the carpeting, had money left over in his budget to burn, or had a brother-in-law in the rug business. At first this crazy talk was annoying, but over the years I came to realize that one of my managing-up functions was to be the one to explain on Jack's behalf that no, the chairman liked beige carpeting, and yes, his favorite flavors of fat-free frozen yogurt were lime and raspberry, and no, he did not forbid the serving of any other flavor in GE facilities.

That last item was one that always made me laugh. With his history of heart problems, Jack is careful about his diet. Fat-free frozen yogurt became his favorite dessert at some point in the 1990s, and he preferred lime and raspberry. He was such a fan, he had food services install frozen yogurt machines in Fairfield and the Crotonville education center. He was like a kid with a new toy, insisting on going into the kitchen and pumping his own, even though he would always dangerously overload the bowl, so much so that they came to be known as the "leaning towers of yogurt." "If I'd had one of these machines as a kid," he told me, "I'd have ruled the neighborhood."

Well, when it came to yogurt he ruled GE. At private luncheons in his conference room, when the dessert menus were presented, a visitor might try to opt for something like the warm apple crisp. "No, no," Jack would say, "you don't want that. Try the fat-free frozen yogurt; it's wonderful." Usually, the visitors knew they were beaten and ordered the yogurt. The same thing would happen at formal dinners, because the GE chef would cleverly rig up a pastry base topped with fat-free frozen yogurt as the primary dessert selection. If you were at his table, it took courage to go with the alternative, chocolate terrine with crème anglaise.

Jack's yogurt tyranny trickled down to the rest of the headquarters operation. Because there were only a couple of yogurt machines, the food service manager decided that they would be set up to serve—you've got it—raspberry and lime, or a twist combining both, since that's what Jack always wanted when he was in the vicinity. During the periods when Jack was away for a week or two, there was much agitation among the staff for other flavors. I suspect that the moment he retired, revolutionaries stormed food services and guillotined the yogurt machine, or at least programmed it so that it would be forever incapable of serving either lime or raspberry.

There was probably a similar insurrection at Crotonville, the scene of one of the more farcical yogurt moments. Jack was teaching there one scorching summer afternoon. After the class broke for the day, he asked for a frozen yogurt. A food service waiter was dispatched across the campus to another building where the yogurt machine was kept, but by the time he returned Jack had been summoned to take an important phone call. For the sake of privacy, he'd shut the door to the office he had borrowed. Afraid to disturb him, the waiter stood outside, and the yogurt turned to soup. The man's supervisor was determined to fill the chairman's order. Undaunted (easy for him to be undaunted, since someone else was rushing around in the heat), he sent the waiter scurrying back for another serving. And when he returned, Jack was still on the phone. Again he was afraid to knock on the closed door. Again the yogurt melted. Before Jack finally got off the phone, the poor waiter had made six round-trips.

Here's a managing-up tip that I could have offered at the time to the waiter and his boss: Knock on the door or change the order to a small bag of pretzels, which Jack likes as much as fat-free frozen yogurt. Just communicate.

Communication Takeaways

- Communication is more than a management tool—it is a catalyst for change.
- Don't be afraid to ask. And then ask again.
- Question yourself constantly; if you don't like your answers, do something about it.
- Be a loudmouth—one whose ideas and messages get spread through every level of your business.
- Nagging doesn't mean you have to be a pain in the neck—but timed correctly, it's very effective.

CHAPTER 14

Teamwork

CAN TEAMWORK FLOURISH in a business organization led by a dynamic, high-profile CEO? Teamwork certainly flourished at GE during Jack Welch's twenty-year tenure as CEO. But I've got to add that it was a customized and hybrid form of teamwork, unique to GE. On some days, the company had the look and feel of an old-fashioned command-and-control hierarchy, particularly when the temperature was hot and the fat-free frozen yogurt was melting. At other times, it did a pretty fair imitation of a Silicon Valley start-up, with an abundance of freewheeling talent, open networks, and caffeinated decision making.

In other words, teamwork functioned as part of an organizational blend that changed frequently as the circumstances and opportunities shifted. Teamwork was a tool—an important tool—but one of many. While the structure flattened out and became less compartmentalized, teams never became an end in themselves. There was still someone upstairs ready, willing, and able to call the shots if necessary.

Teamwork at its best is a blend of old-fashioned command-and-control hierarchy and freewheeling entrepreneurialism.

Jack was savvy enough to keep one foot in the old GE style and the other in the new, more flexible, innovative leadership methods that came into their own in the 1980s and 1990s. At various times, he would adjust the mix—a little more T-shirt entrepreneurial and less pinstripe corporate, or vice versa. Parts of GE could go several months with only limited contact with the CEO's office; others would hear from us weekly or daily. Strong teams were given their head, while weak ones were reined in. There was no hard-and-fast formula. Jack could be a stern taskmaster or a mellow coach depending on what was needed—and what worked.

As deft as he was, GE Corporate never got the hang of the casual Friday beer bashes that were in vogue in the mid-1990s. We tried them a couple of times in the form of picnics on the lawn as a way to build team spirit and build new networks between teams. But people were too busy to spare the time away from the office or didn't see the point of the exercise. The ones I went to were nice in that I could get out to see some friends, yet there wasn't much benefit to be gained casually chatting with a stranger from accounting or some other department, and I got the impression they felt the same way. Theoretically, those gatherings should have had networking benefits, but the support functions of GE's corporate office were so compartmentalized that it was a case of mixing apples and oranges. The interaction didn't hurt, but the payoff was marginal. A program of temporary job swapping or cross training would probably have been more productive.

I'm sure it was different out in the field, where people rubbed shoulders every day and shared a sense of nuts-and-bolts camaraderie. The GE headquarters operation didn't sell, service, or make anything. It functioned in specialized supporting roles, and the interdepartmental personal bonds weren't quite as strong as elsewhere in the company. Surprisingly, there wasn't that much socializing in general. In the upper echelons of management, in fact, while there was personal warmth and respect, relatively limited social interaction took place. With such long hours in the office and on the road, free time was so precious that senior executives tended to head straight home whenever they could.

When he taught at the Crotonville education center, Jack used to ask young executives how much they "celebrated" their accomplishments. He'd hammer away at the need to celebrate as a way to reward themselves and their teammates for a job well done. When I would hear those pep talks, I'd wait until he was back in our office and ask, "When are *we* going to celebrate?" The question was always ignored because the answer was obvious (to him, anyway)—we celebrate every day just by coming to work. As silly as that may sound, there was many a time when we were still in the office as 11 P.M. approached when I hinted that it might be nice to go home, and Jack would give me a reproachful look that said, *Why would you want to go home when we're having so much fun here?*

Don't be afraid to celebrate your successes.

In an important way, that explains why in GE's case a dynamic, high-profile CEO coexisted with teamwork. Jack's teams had fun and derived deep professional satisfaction because they were allowed to make a significant contribution to the company's success. There is a lateral or sideways flow to the input and output of a team that is managing neither up nor down. That's the beauty of teams. At the best of times, they self-manage and cut loose from the constraints imposed by a traditional command-and-control approach to management. Lacking verticality, they must freely circulate resources internally. The team shares strengths and counterbalances weaknesses as it works toward common goals. Jack Welch was as comfortable in that setting as he was at the top of a hierarchy issuing orders downward and receiving compliance upward. He recognized that teams aren't always perfect. The personality blend or talent mix may go awry, or circumstances may change. When that happened, he was willing and able to take charge.

As a leader, Jack had a split personality. But it was an asset, not a liability. His teams had independence, resources, and authority, yet they weren't allowed to drift and dither. If results were not achieved, changes were quickly made in the lineup and the leadership. On one memorable occasion, Jack caught up to Jeff Immelt, who ran GE Medical Systems at the time, by the elevator bank during the annual leadership session in Boca Raton. He proceeded to challenge him about a set of lackluster numbers, and bluntly told Jeff, one of his closest colleagues and a rising star, that he would make changes if the situation didn't improve. (The numbers did recover, and in the biggest change of all, Jeff Immelt went on to become GE's CEO.)

Somehow—and I, frankly, don't know how—Jack managed to convey the impression that he was a member of *every* GE team. Perhaps he did it by traveling in the field, teaching often, and making his presence felt widely throughout the company. But it was not uncommon to get telephone calls and e-mails from GE salespeople trying to arrange for Jack to accompany them on customer visits to close a sale. Not $200 million windfalls, mind you. I'm talking about routine, relatively small or midrange deals. I'd try to let them down gently by explaining how crowded his schedule was; in his personal replies Jack would congratulate them for getting the deal in position to be signed, thank them for the good work, and say that unfortunately he was too busy to join them. We never ignored those requests because they were such vivid reminders of Jack's central role as a GE team member and team builder. It was almost a reflex action: Need help? Call Jack.

And GE business leaders weren't afraid to avail themselves of his services. When truly big deals needed to be nudged toward closure, they'd arrange for him to meet with the customer if he was available or traveling in their area. Jack was also willing to make phone calls to other CEOs to discuss terms that might be causing an impasse at a lower level. This sort of high-level customer contact had some drawbacks. The CEO of one company that was a major customer for GE got in the habit of accumulating complaints about the equipment or service all week and then unloading them on us at six or seven o'clock on a Friday evening. Most of the time, I had to listen to the Friday night complaints and then hunt down somebody in GE to address the man's problems. I got the impression that he had decided that bundling up all the week's complaints and dumping them on Jack's doorstep just as the weekend began was an effective tactic for getting a high-level response. All it accomplished, though, was to postpone a solution for two more days and start my Friday night off on a sour note.

To return to my original question: Can teamwork flourish in a business organization led by a dynamic, high-profile CEO? Yes and no. They are compatible only as long as the CEO can roll up his or her sleeves and give direct support to the company's teams. Otherwise, there's a danger that the larger-than-life CEO will consume the oxygen that the organization needs to keep breathing.

This didn't tend to happen at GE, because Jack insisted on keeping close contact with the teams—contact, but not close management. In other words, he managed down and then stepped back to allow his teams to manage up. As he told author Robert Slater in 1992, "My job . . . is to put the best people on the biggest opportunities and the best allocation of dollars in the right places. That's about it. Transfer ideas and allocate resources and get out of the way."[1]

Get out of the way, but not go away. One of the reasons my job was so challenging and rewarding was that I functioned as one of the principal managing-up contact conduits between the teams and Jack. All I had to do was get out of the way. That he was a de facto member of every team means that I was too. And to a team junkie—I never met a team I didn't want to join—it was a powerful energizer. It seems to me that teams that do not aggressively manage up in order to engage with their senior leaders jeopardize their success by allowing themselves to be marginalized. Our teams had an open invitation to keep in close communication. It was a pleasure to receive e-mails from even the most obscure team leaders working on small tasks deep within the company.

PAYBACK

Back in the mid-1990s, we had to slap together an ad hoc team to get us out of a jam with Wal-Mart. (Speaking of the high-profile CEO, although the legendary Sam Walton died of cancer a few years before, had he still been alive, the situation that I'm about to relate would probably have been handled differently, given his rapport with Jack Welch—or maybe not. Sam Walton could apparently play hardball.)

Every now and then, NBC's *Dateline*, the network's prime-time showcase for investigative reporting, would do a story that would make its parent company, GE, very unhappy. In 1992, *Dateline* correspondent Brian Ross did a story on Wal-Mart's practice of allegedly misrepresenting clothing manufactured in Bangladesh as made in the United States, as well as obtaining these products from factories that employed children for five to eight cents an hour. Wal-Mart management took offense at Ross's report, and someone evidently posted Jack Welch's office phone number on every one of the chain's computer terminals along with the suggestion that employees call Jack to express their outrage. I guess it was a variation on the old adage about taking up your complaints with the organ-grinder instead of the monkey. Except NBC News was no monkey, and it didn't dance to our tune. While GE owned NBC, Federal Communications Commission rules prohibited it from interfering with the network's news coverage.

We were flooded with calls the week before Christmas, that precious period when things are supposed to slow down a little and you can catch up, catch your breath, and finish critical year-end projects. Sue and I drafted two extra staffers to field the calls. We did our best to be civil, but the calls came in such volume that it was all we could do to pick up, listen to the spiel, and cut them off as politely and quickly as possible, hoping that in the momentary interval a non–Wal-Mart call would be able to get through. Many callers didn't even know what they were calling about, just that they were supposed to dial the number and tell us they were angry with GE. The office was a madhouse. Calls came in so fast, they would roll over and block the open lines on the call directors. There wasn't a lull on the phones long enough to get a dial tone to make an outgoing call. Very exasperating! But in a way we were lucky. If the attack had happened anytime other than Christmas week, it might have paralyzed us. As it was, the worst was over by Christmas Eve and the calls trailed off the next week.

Did Wal-Mart make its point? I doubt that there was much of a conversation about it between Jack Welch and Bob Wright, the CEO of NBC. The incident was treated strictly as an issue between Wal-Mart and the television network. Considering Wal-Mart's size and importance as a customer for GE consumer products, I'm probably giving some of my former GE colleagues horrible flashbacks by dredging up the incident in this book. In its own peculiar way, though, the incident supports one of the basic principles of teamwork—build teams that include your customers. And that was the case. Wal-Mart and GE were (and still are) on the same team. Despite the temporary falling-out, the team endured thanks to its inherent strength. Also highlighted by the situation is the need to recognize the fragility of customer-inclusive teams that are as diverse as GE's. As a valued customer, when Wal-Mart teamed up with GE, all the parties involved needed to recognize that a network news operation was also part of the equation. It shouldn't come as a great surprise that news organizations make and break news stories, some of which may involve a GE customer. I think we all knew that—in an abstract way. In 1992, the abstract gave way to a black-and-white Christmas.

GO DIRECTLY TO JAIL

Teamwork, if it is part of the company culture, doesn't even require a formal team. We avoided being caught in a criminal scam several years ago because a woman in GE's employee relocation benefits operation, based in Schenectady, New York, wasn't afraid to call us when something struck her as being a little fishy.

GE has a policy of providing aid to employees who move from place to place over the course of their careers. My colleague's department had been contacted by a man who said he had just been hired to work directly for Jack Welch. He was relocating from out west, he explained, and would need $400,000 to help with a new mortgage he was applying for on a house in Trumbull, Connecticut. The guy knew the local geography, all the procedures, and seemed on the up-and-up.

What we found out later was that his girlfriend had formerly worked at GE, knew about our relocation policy, and had dreamed up a scheme to defraud the company. By posing as someone Jack Welch wanted to hire, the boyfriend thought he had a good chance of flying under the radar. The pair assumed that a midlevel hire would be scrutinized, but not one at the very top. Another assumption was that it would be too dangerous for a bureaucrat in Schenectady to contact headquarters in Fairfield and appear to be questioning the arrangements. Out of the two assumptions, they got half of one right. If company policy had been strictly "What the CEO wants, the CEO gets," the employee benefits people probably would have signed off on the $400,000, no questions asked—only that's not how it worked at GE, and questions were asked. When senior executives hire, they tend to write their own rules. Timidity, however, is not a new GE characteristic, and the people in Schenectady were team players, not bureaucrats.

Mildly surprised that we hadn't informed the benefits operation of a pending hire, one of the supervisors called from Schenectady to check. Mindful of executive prerogatives, she was prepared to hear, "Yes. He's Jack's guy, put it through." But when she asked, ever so gingerly, if Jack Welch was adding someone to his staff, HR didn't punt, ad-lib, or otherwise make up an answer to show that it was in the loop on Jack's plan to expand his operation. Instead, the question was immediately passed on to me. I, of course, knew there was definitely no new hire.

She alerted her bosses, and they went back to the boyfriend to tell him that there was a slight problem—Rosanne. The couple's attempt to explain this away was that Mr. Welch didn't like the way Rosanne handled the situation, so she wasn't involved.

That only made things worse, and in short order led to the hapless couple being arrested, charged, tried, and convicted.

It's easy to see the managing-up angle of this story. The crooks thought that they would exploit the propensity of a big corporation to manage down. The CEO calls the shots, everybody else ducks and covers. But the team in Schenectady managed up by being willing to share information and knowledge, to cross boundaries and ask questions. Teamwork and managing up are synergistic. Empowered, effective teams are capable of systemizing otherwise hit-and-miss managing-up occurrences. Instead of relying on personalities, relationships, and circumstances to produce rather patchy, intermittent instances of managing up, teams institutionalize it. The best ones manage sideways so well (other terms for it are cooperation, coordination, and orchestration), getting the output to flow upward is a simple matter of adjusting the trajectory. In this case, a call to the CEO's office was not a breach of etiquette, it was characteristic of good teamwork that brought a problem and a solution to a higher level.

If managing up isn't taking hold in your organization, it may reflect lackluster teams or a halfhearted commitment to teamwork. The deficiency may start one rung up the ladder from where you are, or be spreading down from the top of the organization.

What should you do? Go to work on your team and make it a model for the rest of your company. Success breeds success.

CRIMINAL INTENT DOWN UNDER

If you controlled petty cash or a bank account in an overseas field operation—let's say Australia—and a man claiming to be from corporate appeared on your doorstep, said he had been mugged, losing his ID, credit cards, and cash, and wanted you to give him a couple of thousand dollars from the company account to buy a ticket back to the United States for an emergency meeting the next day with Jack Welch, what would you do?

Having read the previous anecdote, you're probably thinking, *I would call the CEO's office.*

But. It's three o'clock in the afternoon, roughly three o'clock in the morning in Connecticut. The man's plane leaves in two hours.

Do you hand over the cash? It's only a couple of thousand. Or do you wreck the emergency meeting, strand this important executive, and maybe get reprimanded by high-level people?

Perhaps you're now thinking about passing the buck to one of your subordinates or dumping it on an unsuspecting peer.

Come on, what do you do? The guy needs help, and he's your fellow employee.

I'll tell you what a GE worker in one Australian office did. She called the only twenty-four-hour number at the Fairfield headquarters—security. She asked if Stu Pidd worked for Jack Welch. The guard looked up the name and said, "Nope."

She refused to hand over the money.

This is a true story (although "Stu Pidd" is a made-up name and a bad pun) and, I suspect, a regular scam perpetrated against companies with branch offices in Australia. It was just too pat and perfect to be a one-time occurrence. Again, the bad guy thought he was dealing with an operation that reflexively managed down, and did his best to force a typically managed-down outcome—cover yourself, give him the money.

By now I know you've got the message. Teams share information, knowledge, and skills. Furthermore, they share risk. It was a lot more comfortable to say no after making the call to Fairfield. My Australian coworker formed a team with security in Connecticut, and together they managed up.

HEIR TIME

I've saved the most recent significant example of GE teamwork for last. The process used to select Jeffrey Immelt to succeed Jack Welch as chairman and CEO reinforces my original statements that teamwork can flourish in a business organization led by a dynamic, high-profile CEO, and that teamwork at GE was a hybrid and customized form unique to the company.

Nonetheless, after twenty years at the helm, the process for replacing Jack could have been distracting and damaging to GE. That it wasn't is testament to the depth and breadth of the company's commitment to teamwork.

For starters, Jack devised a process for selecting an heir that preserved the existing team structure. Instead of pulling the likely candidates out of the field and into headquarters, where they could be more closely observed, he left them in place. This way he could avoid the creation of a kind of corporate "war zone," with rivals for the job working in close proximity, each trying to outmaneuver the others. It was a way to keep the peace and to evaluate the candidates on the basis of their day-to-day ability to effectively lead major GE businesses.

Second, he resisted the temptation to take exclusive control of the selection process. Jack used the executive compensation committee of the board of directors as an assessment mechanism, as well as to provide advice and consent. He made sure that the compensation committee especially, and to a lesser extent the entire board, had a chance to get to know each of the candidates and to watch them in action.

We arranged golf foursomes every April in Augusta and again in July in Fairfield so that each candidate (twenty-three of them starting in 1994) would get a chance eventually to play with every board member. As the winnowing got under way, I often wondered whether or not the candidates could tell where they stood according to whom they played golf with. The more likely prospects ended up being repeatedly paired with members of the compensation committee—Jack's selection team—and the least likely were assigned to board members who were not as actively involved. The same pattern prevailed for the seating arrangements at the dinners that followed. Jack and I would carefully mix and match. Afterward, he would seek out the board members for their candid assessments.

At that early stage, none of the candidates had been informed they were on the list. But I think most of them figured it out on their own fairly quickly. You can usually tell when you're being watched, and they were put under a microscope. I can safely say that no other decision in twenty years as CEO so preoccupied Jack as this one did. He thought about it every day for more than six years. He worried that if he blew it and chose the wrong person, much of his legacy could be lost or damaged.

By June 2000, the board, and by that time the press, had narrowed the field to three candidates: Jim McNerney, CEO of Aircraft Engines; Bob Nardelli, CEO of Power Systems; and Jeff Immelt, CEO of Medical Systems. Contrary to press speculation, no candidates from outside GE were seriously considered. The three candidates knew they were final candidates because Jack selected chief operating officers to back them up in each of those three businesses. These COOs were there to ensure a smooth transition in the top management of those businesses. All three candidates knew that the two who were not chosen would be asked to leave the company. Jack felt that the new CEO deserved the right to pick his own executive team and avoid having to work with former rivals who might harbor bitterness at being passed over. All three candidates agreed to this plan.

Getting down to the short list, however, only made the agonizing worse. He probably wouldn't agree with me, but as far as I am concerned, Jack obsessed about the decision in the last six months prior to the final pick. Many people believe that he knew all along whom he would choose. If that was true, he certainly fooled me. Jack and I frequently talked about the three candidates. I never got the feeling that he was leaning toward anyone in particular.

Actually, he talked and I listened. Jack used me as a sounding board to test ideas and reactions. We were careful not to discuss the issue in front of others. Generally, the conversations took place late in the office or in the hallway as we left in the evening. He would relate how one candidate had smoothly handled a presentation or how another might not have asked enough questions at a review session.

Although I always listened closely, my responses were usually noncommittal. And I never asked him straight out who he thought he'd pick. I would have loved to have known, but I wanted to help Jack through the process, and being too nosy would probably have prompted him to clam up. Fortunately for me, I held Jim, Bob, and Jeff in equally high esteem. If I had had a favorite, I know I couldn't have resisted trying to stack the deck a little. As it was, I looked for ways to make life easier for each of them. For example, I remember suggesting that Jeff Immelt revise a planned agenda for the board's visit to Medical Systems. What he had on paper was far too detailed and lengthy. I suggested he try to scale it back before I handed it to Jack to review, which Jeff did.

The board was the first to be informed that Jeff was the choice, and endorsed the decision unanimously on the Friday after Thanksgiving 2000. As is typical for that time of the year on the East Coast, the weather was terrible. We had to get Jeff from South Carolina, where he was spending the holiday with his family, to Palm Beach to meet with Jack and his team from our executive office to prepare for a Monday morning press conference in New York, where the announcement would be made. On Sunday afternoon, Jack left Palm Beach, as the weather deteriorated, to fly to Cincinnati to break the news to Jim, and then go on to Albany to tell Bob. I felt terrible for Jim and Bob, and knew how painful the chore was for Jack. They were good friends, and Bob and Jim were talented leaders, but a choice had to be made.

After the Palm Beach prep session, we flew Jeff to New York using a chartered jet rather than one from the GE fleet in case some journalist's brother-in-law worked at the airport and figured out something was about to happen. Jeff and his wife registered at a New York hotel as Mr. and Mrs. Badowski. Our precautions successfully kept the lid on the story. On Monday morning, Jeff Immelt had his first news conference as GE's CEO-elect.

As I look back on my role during those difficult months and put it into a managing-up context, I was able to function as a sounding board because I was familiar with the ins and outs of the company. I understood the nuances and the dynamics that existed among all the players. Jack had no doubt that what he said to me would be held in strict confidence. That couldn't have happened without a long history of being part of the team. Many companies are too impatient. Teams can get slapped together and revamped overnight. Ours was built to last, and it did. This time, though, I knew that by managing up I was also managing out.

Teamwork Takeaways

- Celebrate—you deserve to recognize accomplishments.
- Take a central role as team member and team builder.
- Get off your pedestal—no job or task should be dismissed as unimportant or not worthy of attention.
- Share *everything*—information, knowledge, skills, risk.

CHAPTER 15

Passion and Purpose

THERE'S AN OLD RULE among poets that if the writer takes care of the sense, the sound takes care of itself. I suggest that you take care of the passion, and the purpose will most certainly take care of itself.

It's a philosophy that's always worked for me. My purpose in writing this book, for example, was to make the passion I felt for my work at GE and with Jack Welch understandable, accessible, and possibly useful to someone else. The best way for me to do that was to stuff this book full of stories drawn from real life. At times, I've wondered whether I shouldn't be loudly nailing lessons and messages to the mast. But I can't give you a purpose, much less provide ready-made passion. All I can do is show mine, what it did and didn't do for me, and inspire others to try whatever makes sense and leads to a purpose they can be proud of.

Do my long days make sense—worrying constantly about screwups, triple-checking everything, being constantly on call?

I suspect that some people would say no, it doesn't. Not for them, anyway.

But look beyond the hard work to the more intangible and in many ways more precious rewards. Does it make sense to earn the right to make a contribution? To make a difference between a done deal and a dead-on-arrival deal? To do a good job? To make friends and to help those friends succeed?

There are no right answers, and only one wrong answer—offering no answer at all. It means you haven't stepped up and made a statement about your passion and purpose. Where there's no passion, there can be no genuine purpose. A paycheck simply isn't enough. Money is not a purpose; and passion for money is nothing but greed.

I'm going to use the rest of this book to tell a few more stories. Will they be about managing up?

You bet. I'll do it with purpose and passion.

HARDBALL TACTICS

Shortly before the GE board decided that Jeff Immelt would be the next CEO of GE, Jack Welch negotiated a small business deal on the side. It was an acquisition, one of hundreds that he made over the years. The negotiations were conducted quietly and involved the usual opening exploratory moves, jockeying for position, offers and counteroffers. But the other side was being difficult. Jack put the pressure on. He wanted an answer. Finally, he called a face-to-face meeting in his conference room.

The two sides squared off. They sat there in silence staring at each other. Minutes passed. More silence. Jack switched on the thousand-yard glare. He meant business.

"Well, you called the meeting—what do you want to say to me?" I asked.

Jack wanted a commitment from me to stay with him in his retirement from GE and work with him as he started his consulting business. When he first broached the subject, I had waffled because I had expected to stay on with the new CEO, and I believe I would have worked well with any of the three remaining candidates for the job. I actually looked forward to it. But in one of his early conversations with Jeff after the decision on an heir was made, Jack informed the CEO-elect that I was not part of the deal. Even though I had yet to sign off, Jack summarily preempted the decision.

But, truth be told, I was ready for a change after thirteen years. Teaming up with Jeff would have provided a different set of challenges and personalities. The arrangement certainly wouldn't have dragged on for another thirteen years—I am a glutton for punishment but would have drawn the line there. I did feel, though, that the chance to help launch the new CEO and make a contribution to the post–Jack Welch era at GE was a purpose that would generate more than enough passion. I was willing to give it three or four more years.

And yet it was difficult—and, in the end, impossible—to give up the purpose that had dominated thirteen years of my life: helping my boss do his job. Still, I fought it. In response, Jack poured on the charm: Life would be easy, more relaxed, less stressful, with half days and short weeks, he promised. He'd only have a few clients, make speeches on college campuses, and spend quality time on the golf course.

Jack was pushing the right buttons, and he knew it. But each time he brought up the subject, I was able to bob and weave enough to avoid giving him a yes-or-no answer. Exasperated, he scheduled one final showdown in the conference room.

We must have sat at the table for close to five minutes staring at each other silently. It was a hardball negotiator's trick, but I wasn't going to be intimidated.

Finally, I broke the silence. "Well, you called the meeting—what do you want to say to me?"

I caught him by surprise. He immediately dropped the tough-guy act and went with his secret weapon, the informal affability and sincerity that's so much a part of his management style, and which is almost impossible to resist. I had made up my mind before the meeting to say yes; even so, I forced him to make his case again. (It never hurts to hear more than once how indispensable you are.)

Nonetheless, I might not have succumbed if the Jack Welch era had simply faded away on schedule by April 2001. But we had one more battle to fight, and we were right in the middle of it soon after our negotiations took place. About a month before the CEO-elect announcement, Jack had launched what the media described as "the biggest industrial acquisition in history." Like Jack and the rest of the company, I had Honeywell fever. So we stayed the course over the next six to eight months, or however long it took to nail down the Honeywell deal.

FINAL SWING

The Honeywell affair was a heartbreaker. We all worked so hard to complete it, and in the end we were left empty-handed.

The whole thing started on October 19, when Jack Welch was interviewed by a CNBC reporter on the floor of the New York Stock Exchange. The newsman asked Jack for his reaction to reports that United Technologies might buy Honeywell.

"It's an interesting idea," he said.

So interesting that about eighteen hours later, GE moved to outbid United Technologies and snatch Honeywell for itself.

The morning after Jack's stock exchange interview, he wanted to talk to Honeywell CEO Mike Bonsignore to let him know an offer was on the way from GE. I got hold of Bonsignore's number two assistant, Debbie Alegreto, whom I had known since she worked for Larry Bossidy, former chairman of Honeywell and previously GE's vice chairman. Debbie told me her boss was meeting with the board and couldn't be disturbed. We found out later that the Honeywell board was just a few minutes away from voting on, and presumably accepting, United Technologies' offer.

"Debbie," I replied, "this is very important. Just take him a note saying that Jack Welch wants to speak with him. Trust me. This is important enough. I'm sure he would want to know about this call. If he doesn't care to take this call, that's okay, but we need to tell him that Mr. Welch would like to speak to him."

Under the law, a corporate board of directors is required to listen to all offers that are made once the company goes on the block. But until our call, Honeywell was unaware of GE's interest and could have properly accepted United Technologies' bid. It probably wouldn't have precluded an eventual offer from GE, but a vote by the board would have complicated the transaction. We knew that if she gave Bonsignore the note, it would have been most unlikely that the vote would go forward. Given the timing, the Honeywell CEO would know immediately what Jack wanted to talk about. He'd have no choice but to postpone the vote.

Debbie couldn't decide.

"Please show him the note. I'll stay on hold." I also told her that if she didn't break into the meeting, Jack Welch was prepared to put out a press release announcing GE's offer to acquire Honeywell.

Debbie delivered the message. When she returned to the phone, she promised that Mr. Bonsignore would call right back, and he did a few minutes later. Jack picked up the receiver and Mike Bonsignore told him the Honeywell board was about to vote.

"Don't," Jack said, "I want to make you a better offer."

And so began the Honeywell adventure—or misadventure.

Passion and purpose drove the Honeywell deal from the start. Jack Welch's purpose as CEO was to build the best, the strongest, and the most profitable GE that he could. His tireless passion grew out of that purpose, and grew to such a degree that it was unthinkable not to take a swing at acquiring Honeywell merely because he was six months away from retirement.

Jack has been faulted by the press and other commentators for overreaching and using the Honeywell deal as an excuse to hang on to power. That's nonsense. He saw a golden opportunity to combine two giant, high-quality corporations into a mammoth enterprise that would have been good—very good—for both sets of shareholders, their workers, customers, and the public. Had he stepped back and not bid, Jack would have betrayed his passion and purpose.

Another criticism was that Jack had been impulsive to make a bid like that on such short notice. But the fact was that GE had already been looking at Honeywell as a possible acquisition, as it does many companies. What's more, our assessments of Honeywell and the benefits of the merger that were hurriedly updated and reviewed on the evening of October 19 and the next morning proved to be accurate. GE and Honeywell would have been a good match—although if I factor in the dramatic stock market decline that occurred after the attack on the World Trade Center in September 2001, and the continued slide in 2002, a GE and Honeywell combination might have proven to be too unwieldy in the business climate that was created.

But that's conjecture. While the initial aftermath of the bid for Honeywell increased the pressure and workload on Jack and me, after a few months the deal had the curious effect of substantially reducing our portfolio of responsibilities. Realizing that managing the acquisition and the early stages of merging the two operations would be an impossible burden for a brand-new CEO, Jack Welch offered to stay past his April 30, 2001, retirement date. The GE board agreed. Jack would continue as CEO, and the "New Guy," as we referred to him, would be designated president and chief operating officer. The COO would, in effect, run the company, while Jack did the heavy lifting on Honeywell. He'd be available for advice and to troubleshoot if need be. Our three main priorities were getting the Honeywell deal nailed down, launching the consolidation of the two companies, and writing Jack's book. Unfortunately, we achieved only one out of three.

DEAL BREAKER

The European Commission formally rejected the merger in early July 2001. The decision capped six months of difficult negotiations. Jack had been caught by surprise when the European Union's competition commissioner, Mario Monti, balked at GE's routine request to expedite the approval process and instead opened a full-scale antitrust investigation. Jack made several trips to Brussels to try to move things along, but prospects for getting the approval slowly unraveled despite his best efforts.

GE went from thinking we would make $30 million or so in concessions, to ease the impact of the merger on a French electronics company, to putting a whopping $2.5 billion in divestitures on the table, most of which involved selling a helicopter engine operation and giving up a huge piece of the company's aviation electronics business in Europe. But even that did not satisfy Monti and Enrique Gonzalez-Diaz, who headed the commission's team handling the investigation of the merger case. Their total demands added up to $5 billion or $6 billion, an amount that shot a huge hole in the economic rationale for the merger.[1]

What fascinated me was the dogged persistence shown by Jack and the rest of his team in pursuing right up to the end a compromise that could have saved the deal. Like the child's punching bag in Chapter 6, they kept getting knocked down again and again, and popping back up. Meanwhile, other teams throughout GE and Honeywell were struggling with the task of blending the two operations together, under the assumption that the merger would be approved (as it had been by the U. S. government). Simultaneously, two separate companies kept doing business as usual. It was an extremely difficult feat of big-league multitasking.

I should add that, through it all, I never heard any grumbling or harsh words about Commissioner Monti. The media tried to portray the situation as a personal confrontation between Mario Monti and Jack Welch. But that wasn't the case. Jack's purpose was to get the deal done, and he pursued it passionately but without rancor. Likewise, Jack did not dump on Gonzalez-Diaz, which would have been applauded by some who saw Gonzalez-Diaz as the prince of darkness and the real instigator of the commission's veto.

I think that Jack's attitude was drawn from his experience in high school and college sports. You don't bad-mouth the referees. You respect the calls, continue to play your best, and accept the outcome—win or lose.

The managing-up message—aside from being careful when you make the largest acquisition in history—is to keep passionately focused on your purpose no matter what kind of surprises come your way. That kind of single-mindedness helps keep your emotions from taking over when unexpected frustrations and disappointments occur. The Honeywell merger made good business sense for both companies. Knowing that, Jack could keep coming back to look for ways to reconfigure the package to make it work to satisfy the European Commission. The moment it stopped making sense—the point when the purpose ceased to exist—he walked away without regret.

THE WRITE STUFF

When the Honeywell deal finally died, Jack Welch was free to become a full-time writer. He had been working on his memoirs off and on for ten months. The Honeywell deal was a major distraction, but with the help of John Byrne, a *Business Week* reporter who had taken a leave of absence from the magazine, the book got done. Without John, Jack would probably still be writing the first chapter.

Jack was very particular in his writing, perhaps because he saw the book as a resource for students of business, rather than merely a mass-market best seller. It was his passion for teaching that truly drove the purpose. (For him, writing the book was its own reward, since Jack's share of his record-breaking advance and all subsequent royalties went to charity.)

At one point, he asked me to take a draft of the manuscript home over the weekend to read—and specifically to check for, in his words, "the bullshit factor." I went through my weekend routine, occasionally ducking into my office to read a few more pages, gleefully writing "BS" in the margin wherever I felt he had lapsed into stilted business jargon. But surprisingly I didn't find very much of it.

A SHORT GOOD-BYE

A few days before Jack turned in the manuscript of his book he began to officially turn over his job. He caught the board of directors by surprise at their July session by announcing that it would be his last as chairman, instead of September, as planned. He was trying to head off the emotional farewell that would have undoubtedly taken place in September. It was classic Jack. He went through the agenda, led the discussion, thanked everyone for their service and support, dropped his bombshell, adjourned the meeting, and walked away.

And he tried to do the same damned thing to Sue and me. On his last day of work in the Fairfield office, when I was busy and not tracking his whereabouts closely, he left for home without a word of farewell. Just skipped out to avoid a scene. We were dumbfounded. When he called in later, I was so steamed, I chewed him out: "It was horrible and unfair to leave the way you did after so many years," I told him. "Your departure this evening gave you a D plus in human relations." He sheepishly agreed to come back the next morning so that the three of us could share a few minutes together, take a few snapshots, and share a memorable and historic moment.

A CITY FALLS SILENT

Jack's elaborately planned book tour was launched with an interview on NBC's *Today* that took place on September 11, only one hour before the first hijacked plane slammed into the World Trade Center just a few miles away. At first we all thought it had been an accident, perhaps involving one of the helicopters that were always buzzing over lower Manhattan. It wasn't long before we realized how wrong we were.

We rushed back to the *Today* offices and spent the rest of the morning the way most of America did, watching TV, horrified and in shock, as history unfolded.

That day, the city of New York was like I have never seen or experienced it before. From the street corner looking south from Rockefeller Center, we could see thick billowing black smoke filling the sky. Traffic moved slowly, if at all, and people on the street seemed to be wandering aimlessly in shock and confusion.

What I remember most was the eerie silence. At one point in the morning, Jack and I were on the street. There were quiet pockets of conversation as people speculated and shared rumors about further attacks. One man, with his young son in tow, stopped Jack and said with anger, "Are you Jack Welch? This is horrible! We just can't let these bastards get away with this."

We ran into Ron Insana, the newscaster from CNBC, who came into the GE building lobby as we were leaving. He was covered from head to toe in a layer of ash and was just arriving to report on what he had seen. Ron had been with us in that same building only the day before doing a business interview. How much can change in one day. We started seeing others on the streets grimy with dust and ash—the subways had been shut down, and obviously they had walked uptown away from the destruction. There had been sketchy early reports on the news, but even without hearing the details we knew the casualties would be catastrophic.

The bridges and tunnels were closed to most traffic. By chance, we were able to catch two cars that had been in the vicinity to bring GE people to Rockefeller Center. Jack and his wife took one car. Pam Wickham of GE Public Relations and I rode home together in the other, in shock and in tears. As the car slowly inched its way through the streets of midtown, I watched the blank faces of the people on the streets staring fixedly ahead—no smiles, no laughter, no conversations. The stunned city was wrapped in a blanket of silence.

Jack's book tour was put on hold until everyone could sort out an appropriate way to move ahead. Since the book's proceeds were going to charity, it strengthened his resolve to carry on. By the middle of October, Jack was on the road for the next couple of months.

Many of our stops were tied in with visits to universities and colleges, where I found myself energized by the enthusiasm of the students. Teacher Jack, of course, ate it up. His question-and-answer sessions often lasted late into the evening. The tour also gave me the chance to meet in person the hundreds of wonderful GE employees I had only dealt with on the phone or in writing. This made me even more proud to be part of the GE family.

A SECOND CAREER

As his book tour wound down, Jack geared up his new career giving corporate speeches—about forty in the first year—and running a one-man consulting firm with several high-profile clients from around the world. I continued on as his chief lieutenant. He brought to his consulting clients the same purpose and passion he had for his job at GE.

Just when I was getting used to this new life, my role expanded once again. Jack's divorce from his second wife, Jane, and his relationship with Suzy Wetlaufer, whom he had met when she interviewed him as an editor at the *Harvard Business Review,* made him front-page news, and overnight I became a crisis PR manager. At the height of the massive press coverage, the office phone rang with media requests nonstop from 7 A.M. to 9 P.M., as well as calls from Jack's friends and associates calling to voice support. The stories in the tabloids had a new twist every day. As with any sensational journalism, Jack and Suzy did the only smart thing—they ignored the press and went on with their lives.

How does all this tie into passion and purpose? Simply this. What you plan for one day can change in the blink of an eye. In that same blink, new opportunities make themselves available all around you. Flexibility and willingness to embrace the opportunities give you an endless runway. I learned from Jack Welch's personality and style to approach each event in my life with passion. Purpose feeds on passion and gives your life meaning.

THE FUN OF MANAGING UP

Over the years, people have approached me wanting to know what it was like to work for Jack Welch. Did he have some secret to success? And that's why I've tried hard to keep the "bow" of this book pointed into the wind of real life.

Was it a smooth fourteen years? No way.

Was it interesting, exhilarating, and rewarding? For sure.

Under the circumstances, managing up was, for me, a survival skill mastered on the job and on the run. But it was not one based on secrets, luck, or genius. For me, managing up came right off the rack, right off the shelf, and right off a list of basic ingredients that are as commonplace as they are priceless:

Chemistry. It's what got us off to a good start and kept us going.

Trust. Trust was what our partnership was built on—and what made our partnership last.

Confidence. The key term to describe Jack—something that propelled his every action.

Impatience. It appears to be a negative, but it gave us the speed to accomplish as much as we did in limited time.

Energy. It kept us buoyant and helped us persevere.

Resilience. The ability to keep going when a roadblock got in the way.

Humor. It made every day fun, no matter what the circumstances.

Common sense. A lifesaver when it came to tough decisions.

Preparedness. This gave us the edge to rise above the pack.

Adaptability. The ability to embrace change.

Simplicity. In other words, keeping things uncomplicated and easy to understand.

Fairness. Treating people in a way we like to be treated.

Communications. The determination to tell the world and each other what was going on.

Teamwork. It let us bring our friends along—they helped us bail out the boat when the water was rising, and they were there in the end for the party.

Passion and purpose. They are what life, and business, are all about.

Together, these fifteen managing-up ingredients produced an extraordinarily effective working partnership—and a whole lot of sheer fun. Yes, there I go again—fun. If work isn't fun, there's something wrong. Well-paid drudgery is still drudgery. It's painful and demeaning. By managing up you make an investment that pays a handsome dividend in satisfaction and self-respect.

CHAPTER 1

1. *The Wizard of Oz* (screenplay), written by Florence Ryerson and Edgar Allan Wolfe; *Bartlett's Familiar Quotations,* 16th edition (Boston: Little, Brown, 1992), p. 515.

CHAPTER 3

1. *Webster's Third New International Dictionary* (Springfield, Mass.: Merriam, 1981), p. 475.

CHAPTER 4

1. John F. Welch Jr. with John A. Byrne, *Jack: Straight from the Gut* (New York: Warner Business Books, 2001), pp. 218–19.

2. Robert Frost, *The Complete Poems of Robert Frost* (New York: Holt, Rinehart and Winston, 1964), p. 268.

CHAPTER 5

1. Peter F. Drucker, *The Effective Executive* (New York: HarperBusiness, 1996), p. 42.
2. Welch, *Jack*, p. 155.

CHAPTER 6

1. Welch, *Jack*, p. 259.

CHAPTER 7

1. Welch, *Jack*, p. 212.
2. "The most wasted day is that in which we have not laughed." Chamfort, *Maxims et pensées*, in *The International Thesaurus of Quotations*, compiled by Rhoda Thomas Tripp (New York: Harper and Row, 1970), p. 342.

CHAPTER 9

1. I've drawn on two sources to explain Six Sigma: John F. Welch, Jr., *Jack*, pp. 328–29, and Michelle Conlin, "Revealed at Last: the Secret of Jack Welch's Success," *Forbes*, January 26, 1998, p. 44.

CHAPTER 11

1. William Shakespeare, *Henry VI, Part 2*, act 4, scene 2, II. 76–77.

CHAPTER 12

1. Welch, *Jack*, p. 210.
2. Francis Hesselbein and Paul M. Cohen, editors, *Leader to Leader* (New York: Drucker Foundation Leaderbooks, 1999), p. 233. This anthology excerpts a passage from Max De Pree's *Leadership as an Art*, dealing with a leader's role in defining reality and saying thank you.

CHAPTER 14

1. Robert Slater, *The New GE: How Jack Welch Revived an American Institution* (Homewood, Ill.: Business One Irwin, 1993), p. 167.

CHAPTER 15

1. "How Jack Fell Down: Inside the Collapse of the GE Honeywell Deal," *Time*, July 16, 2001, p. 40.

The creation of this book, from its very first word to the final and inevitable edit, is due to many more friends, colleagues, and acquaintances than I can acknowledge here. But there are some to whom I owe a particular debt of gratitude for their help, support, and professionalism throughout the writing process.

First and foremost, I thank my parents, who gave me the values that made me who I am. It was those values that carried me through a successful career and ultimately led to the writing of this book.

If I hadn't received that phone call from literary agent Margaret McBride nearly three years ago, you wouldn't be reading this today. She outlined an idea that won me over. Doubleday's Roger Scholl, Stephanie Land, and the Random House team had the confidence to see the project through to its end. And what would I have done without Roger Gittines? He has been my writer and honorary psychiatrist for two long years. I thank him for his patience in piecing together a ton of disconnected thoughts. My Saturday mornings will never be the same.

My brother, Ray; sister-in-law, Patti; niece, Cheryl; and nephew, Steven, have graciously put up with my overdedication to my work. Their support, along with that of my large extended family, has been wonderful. They, along with a network of aunts, uncles, and cousins (too many to mention), have been the best example of a loving, harmonious family. Four cousins in particular—Susan, Mary Ann, Noreen, and Mary Ann P.—are the best friends a girl could ask for.

When I had doubts about writing the book, Kathy Lorenz gave me the confidence to go for it, Dan Arenovski did more than his share of listening to all of my stories—book-related and otherwise—and Bill Lane provided great editing advice.

It's impossible to name all of the GE employees who have touched my life. Kathy Hanson, whom I met in the elevator on the first day of our new GE assignments back in 1977, has shared my most difficult and most joyous moments over the last twenty-five years. She gets my soul-sister award. Personal friends Kathy Harris, Vickie Moran, and Ann Vitale, will always be special to me, but it was every one of the other employees in Fairfield (particularly the "girls in the hood") and in the GE businesses around the world that I worked with every day who made my job easier and also a lot of fun. I won't try to list them all—I wouldn't be able to live with myself if I forgot someone—but without their support, I would not be writing phrases like "I love my job."

Whenever I told a story of what happened in the office and used "I," often it was really "we." The other half of the "we" was Sue Baye, the epitome of loyalty, dedication, and friendship. We sat twelve feet apart for thirteen years. That's usually not an easy thing to do, but in our case it was. You name it, we shared it and laughed about it. If you need an example of how to bond with your co-workers, check us out—what a team we were. I thank her for all she's done for me.

And what could I say about Jack Welch? This book talks about chemistry and developing a great working relationship. These are just attempts at explaining a little bit about what happened. There is no explanation for our relationship other than I love the guy and everything about him. I could not find a better mentor, teacher, and friend. Jack, thanks for the entertainment—thanks for everything.

© Misencik Photography

ROSANNE BADOWSKI worked on the administrative support staff at GE for more than twenty-five years, thirteen of them as the executive assistant to the CEO and Chairman, Jack Welch. When Welch retired in September 2001 and established a private consulting firm, Badowski joined him as his principal lieutenant and chief of staff. She lives in Boston.

ROGER GITTINES is a writer based in Washington, D.C.